Lifting the Oil Curse

Improving Petroleum Revenue Management in Sub-Saharan Africa

Menachem Katz, Ulrich Bartsch, Harinder Malothra, and Milan Cuc

International Monetary Fund
Washington, DC

©2004 International Monetary Fund

Production: IMF Multimedia Services Division
Cover Design: Luisa Menjivar
Cover Photos: Corbis (right) and Holger Floerkemeier for the IMF (left)
Typesetting: Alicia Etchebarne-Bourdin

Cataloging-in-Publication Data

Lifting the oil curse: improving petroleum revenue management in Sub-Saharan Africa /
Menachem Katz . . . [et al]. — Washington, D. C. : International Monetary Fund, 2004.

       p.   cm.

     ISBN 1-58906-317-1
     Includes bibliographical references.

I. Africa, Sub-Saharan — Economic policy. 2. Fiscal policy — Africa, Sub-Saharan. 3. Petroleum
industry and trade — Africa, Sub-Saharan. I. Katz, Menachem, 1946–

HC800.L43 2003

Price: $20.00

Please send orders to:
International Monetary Fund, Publication Services
700 19th Street, NW, Washington, DC 20431, U.S.A.
Telephone: (202) 623-7430   Telefax: (202) 623-7201
Internet: http://www.imf.org

Contents

Tables

Preface

With increasing international interest in the oil to be found off Africa's western and southern coast, there is also intensified scrutiny of the reasons for the disappointing economic performance of the oil-producing countries in the region during the last two to three decades. The question is how to turn oil revenue into a blessing, rather than the curse it may have been in many oil-based economies. This paper discusses the latest thinking on best-practice institutions and policies, compares this with current practice in the African oil-exporting countries, and presents a way forward, taking into account African policymakers' concerns.

This Special Issues Paper is based on a background paper prepared for a workshop on macroeconomic policies and governance in sub-Saharan African countries held jointly by the African Department (AFR) of the IMF and the Oil and Gas Policy Unit and the Africa Region of the World Bank, during April 29–30, 2003, in Douala, Cameroon. The workshop brought together high-level policymakers from Angola, Cameroon, Chad, the Democratic Republic of the Congo, the Republic of Congo, Equatorial Guinea, Gabon, Nigeria, and São Tomé and Príncipe, including ministers of finance, ministers of oil, governors of central banks, and heads of national oil companies, as well as IMF and Bank staff. This paper also takes into account African policymakers' concerns and suggestions as expressed during the workshop.

The paper reflects the contributions of several staff members in the African Department. In particular, the authors are grateful to Magnus Alvesson, Rodolphe Blavy, Deborah Malama Chungu, Jean-François Dauphin, Mansour Ndiaye, and Joseph Ntamatungiro. We also benefited greatly from comments and suggestions from Rolando Ossowski of the IMF's Fiscal Affairs Department, Charles McPherson from the World Bank, and numerous other reviewers. We would also like to acknowledge the help provided by Marie-Jeannette Ng Choy Hing in document preparation, and thank Tom Walter from African Department and Sean M. Culhane of the External Relations Department for editing the paper and coordinating the production of the publication.

1 Introduction

Over the last decade, the Atlantic Ocean off the coast of western and southern Africa has become one of the most promising oil-exploration areas in the world. Six countries in the area are by now well-established oil producers, and more are to join their ranks in the near future. Oil-producing countries are faced with some of the same challenges as other natural resource–based countries, but their difficulties seem to be accentuated by the peculiar nature of oil markets and oil production. The main challenges come from the high volatility of oil prices, the enclave nature of the oil sector, the exhaustibility of oil reserves, and the high concentration of revenue flows from the oil sector, which invites rent-seeking behavior and may lead to governance problems. In the past, many oil-producing countries have been disappointed in their expectations that favorable resource endowments would lead to rapid improvements in development indicators. This paper focuses on the policies that have been and should be implemented by the oil-producing countries. It summarizes proceedings of the Workshop on Macroeconomic Policies and Governance in Sub-Saharan African Oil-Exporting Countries, hosted jointly by the African Department of the International Monetary Fund and the Africa Region and the Oil and Gas Policy Unit of the World Bank. The workshop brought together high-level policymakers from African oil-producing countries during April 29–30, 2003, in Douala, Cameroon.

The paper discusses macroeconomic and oil sector policy, and governance issues in the six oil-producing countries—Angola, Cameroon, the Republic of Congo, Equatorial Guinea, Gabon, and Nigeria—as well as the newcomer Chad, which had started production by mid-2003. The main objectives are to (1) give an overview of the general policy issues in oil-producing countries, (2) describe actual practice in the countries, and (3) discuss African policymakers' perspectives and an agenda for further discussions. Issues of policy formulation related to the oil sector will be discussed in eight sections, in line with the workshop agenda, after a general introduction of economic indicators in Chapter 2. The following four sections describe macroeconomic policy issues, under the headings macroeconomic policy (Chapter 3); fiscal policy formulation (Chapter 4); persistent surpluses and accumulation of assets (Chapter 5); and exchange rate regimes and competitiveness (Chapter 6). These are followed by two sections on governance issues, namely, institutional oversight of the oil sector (Chapter 7) and transparency requirements (Chapter 8). The concluding section presents a summary of relevant policy issues. In each section of the paper, a general background discussion lists issues to be considered in policy formulation. This is followed by a description of current practice in the countries as seen by Bank and IMF staff, and a third subsection consisting of policy recommendations, together with a summary of the discussions during the Douala workshop with African policymakers.

2 Country Overview

The seven countries in the group of oil-producing African countries together produced an average of 3.8 million barrels of oil per day in 2001, equivalent to 5 percent of world oil production. Their total production is projected to increase to an average of 5 million barrels per day by 2006. In the past, Nigeria, Angola, and Gabon were the three biggest oil producers in the region, but Gabon is projected to fall behind both Equatorial Guinea and the Republic of Congo (see Figure 1 for an overview of oil production and exports in this group of countries between 1990 and 2006). Oil exports in the region totaled more than US$25 billion per year in the period 1997–2001 and are estimated to increase to $30 billion during 2002–06.

The countries show enormous differences in population size (Nigeria's population of 130 million is 260 times that of Equatorial Guinea) and their degree of reliance on oil in terms of GDP (oil exports were valued at 96 percent of GDP in Equatorial Guinea and only 11 percent in Cameroon in 2001—see Figure 2, top panel). Yet in terms of administrative capacity, human resources, and living standards, the countries share many of the features of other developing countries.

Table 1 provides an overview of development performance for the countries in the group and compares this performance with indicators for sub-Saharan Africa (SSA) as a whole. In general, oil-producing countries in Africa have not achieved better social indicators than other African countries. In terms of per capita GDP, only Gabon and Equatorial Guinea rank significantly above the SSA average. Infant mortality in 2000 was higher in three countries in the group than in the SSA average. Only Cameroon, the Republic of Congo, Nigeria, and Gabon reduced infant mortality rates below the SSA average. Life expectancy at birth was lower in the Republic of Congo than the average for sub-Saharan Africa and about the same as the average in Angola and Nigeria. Only in Cameroon, Equatorial Guinea, and Gabon was it noticeably higher. Oil-producing countries also have not achieved higher literacy rates than SSA countries on average. The SSA oil-exporting countries have also performed worse than other oil-exporting countries. Table 2 shows that out of 32 oil-exporting countries worldwide, 6 of the 9 countries with the lowest human development indicators are in sub-Saharan Africa.

3

Figure 1. Oil Production, Exports, and Government Revenue, 1990–2006

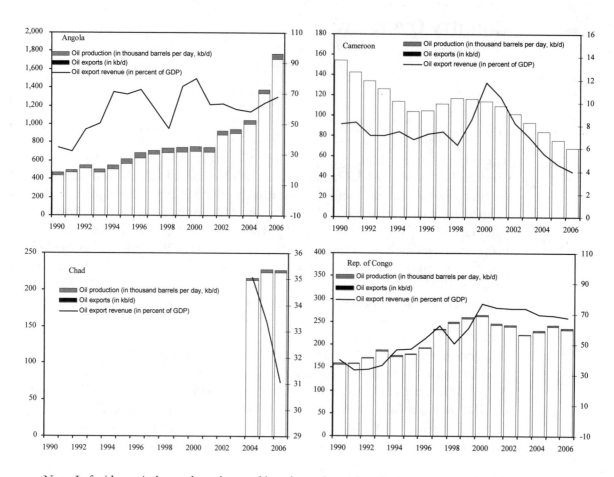

Note: Left-side vertical axes show thousand barrels per day; right-side show percent of GDP.

Governments in the group are highly dependent on oil revenue. On average, oil revenue constituted 68 percent of total government revenue in 2001, a share that is projected to decline slightly to 57 percent during 2002–06 (see Figure 3 for oil revenues in 2001). Government oil revenue amounted to 20 percent of the combined GDP of the region. All countries in the group with the exception of Cameroon and Chad depend heavily on oil revenue, with at least two-thirds of

Figure 1 *(concluded)*

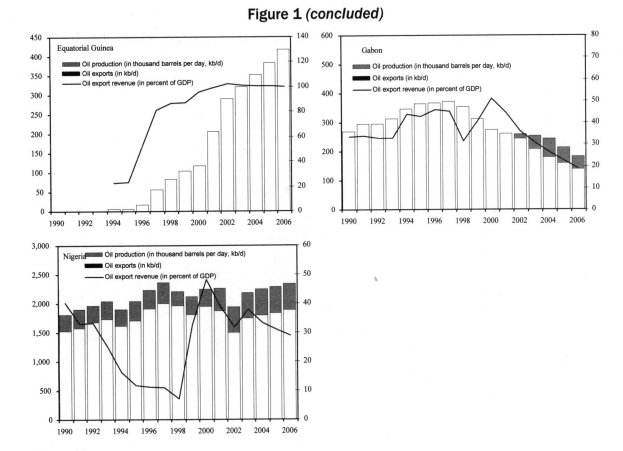

Sources: Country authorities; and IMF staff estimates.
Note: Left-side vertical axes show thousand barrels per day; right-side show percent of GDP.

total government revenue coming from oil. Of the established oil producers, Cameroon has the most diversified revenue base, and the share of oil in total revenue is projected to decline from an average of 26 percent during 1997–2001 to 16 percent during 2002–06. Regarding taxation of the oil sector, the governments collected about 50 percent of the total export value of oil on average during 2001, ranging from 90 percent in Nigeria to 21 percent for Equatorial Guinea.[1]

---

[1]Government revenue in Nigeria is gross revenue, that is, before the payment of the national oil company share in joint-venture operating and capital costs. The large government take, therefore, goes along with exposure to exploration and development risks.

Figure 2. Oil Exports and Government Revenue, 2001

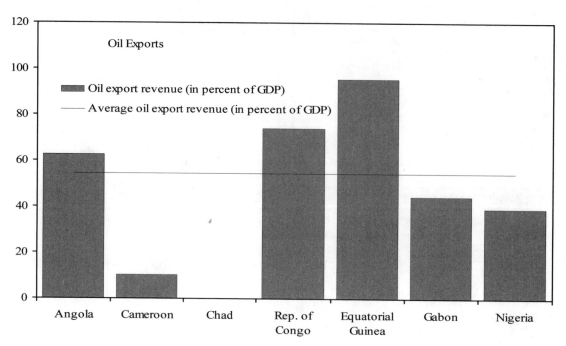

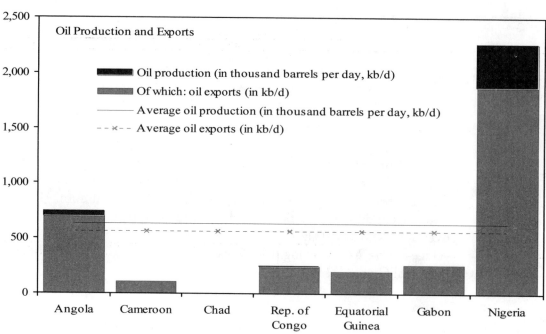

Sources: Country authorities; and IMF staff estimates.

6

Table 1. Oil-Producing Countries in Africa: Selected Economic Indicators, 1960–2000

	Angola					Cameroon				
	1960	1970	1980	1990	2000	1960	1970	1980	1990	2000
Economic development										
Nominal GDP per capita (in U.S. dollars)	...	492.1	776.2	1,027.8	664.5	...	154.1	774.7	967.7	577.7
GDP per capita, PPP (in U.S. dollars) 1/	...	783.9	1,281.7	1,676.7	2,091.7	...	511.1	1,258.4	1,994.1	2,120.4
Social indicators										
Mortality rate, infant (per 1,000 live births)	206.0	178.2	153.8	130.2	127.6	161.2	125.8	102.6	81.0	75.8
Life expectancy at birth, total (years)	33.2	37.2	41.2	45.5	46.6	39.5	44.6	50.0	54.2	50.0
Illiteracy rate, adult total (percent of people ages 15 and above)	...	...	...	...	...	...	68.7	53.2	37.5	24.2
Oil and non-oil sectors										
Oil revenue (percent of total govt revenue)					89.4				33.7	31.7
Fuel exports (percent of merchandise exports)	3.0	13.4	78.0	93.5	...	0.0	0.0	30.7	49.9	35.0
Food imports (percent of merchandise imports)	19.3	15.7	18.4	...	...	18.5	12.2	8.6	18.5	18.9

	Chad					Rep. of Congo				
	1960	1970	1980	1990	2000	1960	1970	1980	1990	2000
Economic development										
Nominal GDP per capita (in U.S. dollars)	...	72.0	147.9	285.7	188.0	...	...	559.9	244.5	95.9
GDP per capita, PPP (in U.S. dollars) 1/	...	278.4	423.0	816.3	1,054.3	...	366.3	923.7	1,719.7	1,854.9
Social indicators										
Mortality rate, infant (per 1,000 live births)	193.4	171.2	123.0	118.0	101.2	152.2	131.0	112.2	95.8	84.9
Life expectancy at birth, total (years)	34.9	38.2	42.2	46.2	48.5	41.4	45.2	49.0	51.5	45.7
Illiteracy rate, adult total (percent of people ages 15 and above)	...	90.7	83.3	72.3	57.4	...	77.2	65.9	52.5	38.6
Oil and non-oil sectors										
Oil revenue (percent of total govt revenue)	0.0	0.0	0.0	0.0	0.0				58.0	77.4
Fuel exports (percent of merchandise exports)	4.0	0.1	0.0	...	...	...	0.2	8.0	...	...
Food imports (percent of merchandise imports)	16.4	20.6	23.0	...	...	...	15.7	9.4	...	...

	Equatorial Guinea					Gabon				
	1960	1970	1980	1990	2000	1960	1970	1980	1990	2000
Economic development										
Nominal GDP per capita (in U.S. dollars)	...	129.6	116.9	379.3	3,039.9	...	1,097.6	5,621.5	6,400.2	4,213.9
GDP per capita, PPP (in U.S. dollars) [1]	...	315.2	623.1	910.9	6,032.5	...	2,306.3	4,423.2	6,453.3	7,277.9
Social indicators										
Mortality rate, infant (per 1,000 live births)	187.0	164.0	142.4	121.0	101.8	169.4	137.2	104.4	71.6	58.0
Life expectancy at birth, total (years)	36.9	39.9	43.2	47.2	51.0	40.9	44.2	48.2	51.9	52.7
Illiteracy rate, adult total (percent of people ages 15 and above)	...	54.0	40.0	26.7	16.8	...	...	...	...	...
Oil and non-oil sectors										
Oil revenue (percent of total govt revenue)					83.5				45.8	67.5
Fuel exports (percent of merchandise exports)	...	...	...	...	...	...	42.6	87.9	89.3	...
Food imports (percent of merchandise imports)	...	...	36.4	...	...	...	14.3	19.1	19.4	...

	Nigeria					Sub-Saharan Africa				
	1960	1970	1980	1990	2000	1960	1970	1980	1990	2000
Economic development										
Nominal GDP per capita (in U.S. dollars)	...	120.3	913.3	314.2	324.1	473.4	609.0	658.4	587.4	564.4
GDP per capita, PPP (in U.S. dollars) 1/	...	249.9	573.4	777.3	956.6	...	814.1	1,122.2	1,453.0	1,683.2
Social indicators										
Mortality rate, infant (per 1,000 live births)	188.6	139.4	99.4	86.4	84.4	164.0	138.2	115.6	102.5	91.2
Life expectancy at birth, total (years)	39.7	42.9	45.8	49.1	46.8	40.2	44.2	47.6	50.0	46.5
Illiteracy rate, adult total (percent of people ages 15 and above)	...	79.9	67.1	51.4	36.1	...	72.0	61.9	50.2	38.5
Oil and non-oil sectors										
Oil revenue (percent of total govt revenue)	...	26.3	81.1	72.6	82.2	...	...	...	...	...
Fuel exports (percent of merchandise exports)	...	58.1	96.9	96.6	99.6	...	15.6	26.6	27.9	28.4
Food imports (percent of merchandise imports)	...	8.3	15.1	6.4	20.2	...	10.8	9.7	...	10.3

Sources: IMF, 2002, *World Economic Outlook (WEO)*, Washington, and World Bank, 2002, *World Development Indicators(WDI)*, Washington.

[1] PPP refers to purchasing power parity.

Table 2. Human Development Indices (HDI) for Oil-Producing Countries, 2001

Country	HDI Value 2000	HDI Rank	Country	HDI Value 2000
Norway	0.942	87	Turkmenistan	0.741
Brunei Darussalam	0.856	88	Azerbaijan	0.741
Bahrain	0.831	98	Iran, Islamic Rep. of	0.721
Kuwait	0.813	106	Algeria	0.697
United Arab Emirates	0.812	110	Indonesia	0.684
Trinidad and Tobago	0.805	111	Equatorial Guinea	0.679
Qatar	0.803		**Developing countries**	**0.654**
Mexico	0.796	115	Egypt	0.642
Malaysia	0.782	117	Gabon	0.637
Russian Federation	0.781	135	Cameroon	0.512
Libyan Arab Jamahiriya	0.773	136	Rep. of Congo	0.512
Venezuela	0.770	139	Sudan	0.499
Saudi Arabia	0.759		**Sub-Saharan Africa**	**0.471**
Oman	0.751	148	Nigeria	0.462
Kazakhstan	0.750		**Least developed countries**	**0.445**
Ukraine	0.748	161	Angola	0.403
		166	Chad	0.365

Source: United Nations Development Program (UNDP).
Note: Sub-Saharan African oil-exporting countries are highlighted.

Figure 3. Oil Revenues and Government Deficits, 2001

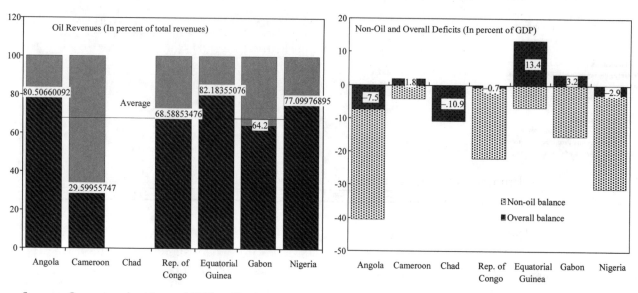

Sources: Country authorities; and IMF staff estimates.

3 Macroeconomic Policy Challenges

A. Background Discussion

Macroeconomic policy in oil countries faces challenges arising from three characteristics of oil revenue: (1) oil revenue is more volatile than revenue from other export commodities because of international market conditions; (2) oil revenue is a foreign exchange inflow, and its use can have large effects on macroeconomic stability and economic structure; and (3) oil is an exhaustible resource with a finite revenue stream. The challenge of macroeconomic policy in SSA oil countries is to stabilize budgetary expenditures and sterilize excess revenue inflows in the context of medium- to long-term sustainability considerations, and thereby provide an environment conducive to growth and poverty reduction. In most of the oil-producing countries, there has been a strong deficit bias, and a procyclical fiscal policy has been driven by oil price developments.

Oil revenue volatility

Empirical investigations have shown that oil prices are more volatile than prices of other commodities.[2] Fiscal policy, therefore, has to attempt to insulate the economy from the volatility of oil revenues, because frequent upward or downward adjustments of fiscal expenditures are costly. Volatility in budgetary spending hurts the economy through uncertainty about aggregate demand and through costs associated with factor reallocations. The "boom-bust" cycles

---

[2]See Engel and Valdés (2000).

induced by frequent adjustments of budgetary expenditure are not conducive to private sector activity. In addition, if expenditures become entrenched, cuts may not be possible in some line items, and prioritizing budget cuts becomes increasingly difficult. If expenditure cannot be cut sufficiently, governments may be forced to borrow, and borrowing costs may be inversely related to oil prices. (Borrowing is easier when oil prices are high).[3]

Attempts at stabilizing budgetary expenditure suffer because oil price projections are unreliable. In fact, various studies have shown that the profile of oil prices over the past 30 years can best be described as a random walk process.[4] This implies that the best predictor of tomorrow's price is today's price and that the prediction can be spectacularly wrong.[5] However, periods of relative price stability have also been observed.

Given the high uncertainty about future oil prices, fiscal policy should aim at accumulating precautionary savings in the form of foreign financial assets in years with high oil revenues, which could then serve to finance deficits in years with revenue shortfalls. However, it should be recognized that large market downturns and a depletion of the assets of such stabilization funds are always possible. Policymakers in the past mostly believed that a market downturn would be short-lived, whereas high oil prices were thought to be the norm. They therefore did not adjust expenditure downward in times of low oil prices until forced to by borrowing constraints.

In addition to stabilization funds, other ways to safeguard against the possibility of revenue shortfalls may be needed. One such way is to broaden the revenue base through economic diversification. Another approach would be for the government to target persistent fiscal surpluses in order to create financial assets as precautionary savings. Interest income from these assets would augment government revenue and would reduce overall volatility in government revenue. Hedging against oil price fluctuations on international commodity exchanges is another possible way to reduce volatility.[6]

---

[3]See Hausmann and Rigobon (2002).

[4]Engel and Valdés (2000).

[5]Since the 1970s, very large price swings have been brought on by unforeseen elements. Examples include the Iranian revolution in 1979, which cut oil supplies by 3 million barrels per day; the switch from price policy to market share policy by Saudi Arabia in 1985; and the occupation of Kuwait in 1990, followed by its swift end in 1991.

[6]For an overview of possibilities for hedging, see Daniel (2001).

Foreign exchange inflow from oil

Oil is normally produced in an "enclave," with high capital and low labor intensity, and the bulk of production is exported. Export proceeds are received in U.S. dollars, and the government's share of these proceeds is a foreign exchange inflow into the economy. The domestic use of the foreign exchange inflow generally leads to an appreciation of the real effective exchange rate (REER) and a loss of competitiveness in the non-oil tradables sector of the economy.[7] The economic structure would therefore shift away from the production of tradable goods, labor and capital would move into the nontradable sectors, and imports would rise.

This structural change resulting from the use of oil revenue has been called the "Dutch disease"; it is not necessarily problematic, although fast structural change can be accompanied by economic and social dislocations. Another issue is the sustainability of the aggregate demand structure in light of the volatility and exhaustibility of oil revenue. When oil revenue falls, production and consumption patterns may become incompatible with the availability of foreign exchange, unless sufficient public and/or private savings have been accumulated during the good times. A fiscal policy designed to keep domestic demand stable in the face of fluctuating oil revenues will tend to dampen real exchange rate appreciation and its detrimental effects on competitiveness.

If stability of government spending and domestic demand in general can be maintained, the need for supply-side adjustment will diminish correspondingly, and short- to medium-term reallocation costs will be minimized. If fiscal policy is also aimed at long-term sustainability, the assets accumulated during the lifetime of the oil fields ensure that the foreign exchange inflow compatible with consumption and production patterns continues even after the depletion of oil reserves. The desire to limit real exchange rate appreciation provides another argument in favor of accumulating income-producing foreign assets: to sterilize the foreign exchange inflow from the oil sector (see also Section 6 on exchange rate issues). Government policies that encourage private sector saving—greater reliance on indirect taxation, pension reform, reform of the banking system, and reduced business profit taxes—can complement fiscal policy in moderating real exchange rate appreciation.

---

[7]If oil revenue is relatively unimportant in the economy and the factors of production are underemployed prior to the oil boom, aggregate demand expansion does not necessarily lead to appreciation.

Exhaustibility of oil

Oil is a nonrenewable resource. It constitutes national wealth that can be approximated by the present value of the rent earned in its production (essentially proceeds from projected future sales after deduction of relevant extraction costs).[8] Using the principle of intergenerational equity, one can argue that this national wealth should be used in a manner that will leave future generations at least as well off as the current one. This is a savings motive in addition to the precautionary and sterilization motives discussed above.[9] However, uncertainty over reserves, future oil prices, the return on financial or physical assets, and society's discount rate means that it is nearly impossible to calculate how much should be saved during the lifetime of the oil reserves. Hence, the accumulation decision can have an element of value judgment.

However, it can be argued that governments, rather than investing the oil revenue proceeds in financial assets, should use them to finance public expenditure that "crowds in" private investment and to reduce taxes as far as possible to eliminate distortions and disincentives. This is particularly important in countries where there is an urgent need to build up infrastructure and provide essential services. This course of action would support non-oil growth and would create a larger revenue base in the future; fiscal sustainability could thus be ensured with a modest increase in tax rates when oil revenue trails off, and interest earnings from a savings fund would not be needed. The present generation would use up the natural resource wealth but would leave to future generations compensating man-made wealth.

In practice, the decision about the form of asset accumulation—financial versus real—under a policy that seeks to ensure equitable treatment of all generations needs to balance often-competing considerations. The fact that severe absorptive capacity constraints exist in African oil-producing countries, and that the efficiency of public spending among at least some of them has been low, would suggest that a large portion of oil revenue savings should be invested in financial assets. Conversely, the widespread poverty and low human development indicators in many oil-producing countries would argue in favor of upgrading

---

[8]Profits accruing to foreign-owned companies also need to be excluded from the calculation of the national oil wealth.

[9]In principle, we could let private households decide how much of the oil revenue to save for future generations. But they might not take the macroeconomic effects of their collective actions sufficiently into account, and intervention might still be necessary to sterilize the foreign exchange inflow.

domestic infrastructure and increasing the level of public services as a way of improving the quality and productivity of physical and human capital.[10]

B. Current Practice

African oil-producing countries commonly do not follow any declared fiscal rule, with the exception of Cameroon, where a balanced budget is implicitly targeted (see Table 3 for a summary of this section). Budgets are usually prepared on the basis of a projected oil price, and ad hoc adjustments to budgets are common. Equatorial Guinea and Chad are moving toward the projection of fiscal surpluses and the accumulation of assets. The former is currently the only country in the group where oil revenue clearly exceeds the country's absorptive capacity and where sizable foreign assets have been accumulated, and the latter may find itself in a similar position, at least during the initial years of oil production. Cameroon has provisions in place under the Poverty Reduction and Growth Facility (PRGF)-supported program to save unprogrammed windfalls when oil prices and government oil revenues surpass budgetary projections, although these have so far not been implemented. Nigeria accumulated reserves in the past as part of an "oil fund," but this fund was embezzled and the practice was discontinued.

Following the oil booms, Nigeria experienced large increases in public spending and fiscal deficits that fueled macroeconomic volatility. Nigeria's budget deficit increased dramatically from the early 1970s onward as expenditures rose faster than revenues. In periods of high oil prices, public expenditure was allowed to rise substantially, while there was little ability to reduce spending in periods of low oil prices. The federal government deficit has remained above 4 percent of GDP for most years since 1975, and sometimes substantially higher. This "ratchet effect," stemming from an irreversible rise in expenditures when oil revenue was high, has been a major contributing factor to the accumulation of a large public sector debt. Figure 4 compares oil revenue, fiscal expenditure, and the overall fiscal balance for Nigeria, Venezuela, and Indonesia. Indonesia was successful in stabilizing fiscal spending, whereas in Nigeria and Venezuela oil price and oil revenue volatility was transmitted to the economy through volatility in public spending.

---

[10]The strategy of sharing the oil wealth across generations is taken here as given. Emergency humanitarian conditions in some of the countries in certain periods—for example, the Congo after the civil war—are likely to lower the priority given to intertemporal equity considerations.

Table 3. Current Practice in Fiscal Policy

Country	Fiscal Rules	Integrity of Budget	Earmarking	Intergenerational Equity Provisions
Angola	None.	Oil revenue (excluding bonuses) and expenditures are included in the budget. Bonuses are paid to Sonangol and, in some cases, directly to various autonomous social funds.	None.	None.
Cameroon	Target a balanced budget at the expected level of oil revenues. A contingency mechanism lowers the target in case of a shortfall.	All oil revenue is included in the budget.	None.	Ongoing discussions to set up a Fund for Future Generations (FFG).
Chad	Target a fiscal surplus at the projected oil price and deposit a fixed percentage of oil revenue in an FFG.	All oil revenue should be fully budgeted and associated spending should follow normal budgetary procedures.	Net direct oil revenue (after debt service to the World Bank and allocations for FFG) is to be spent mainly in priority sectors for poverty reduction; namely, health, education, rural development, and infrastructure.	Yes. The exact rules guiding the eventual use of this fund have not yet been agreed upon, and should be designed so as to ensure inter-generational equity.
Republic of Congo	None.	Oil revenue and expenditures are included in the budget. Effective unified management of treasury operations is impaired by collateralized debt operations and financing of some public investment projects directly with oil revenues.	Proportion of oil revenues earmarked for specific uses—collateralized debt-service payments and investment projects—account for 40 percent of total oil fiscal revenue in 2001.	None.
Equatorial Guinea	None. The revised budget for 2002 projects a large fiscal surplus (including oil revenue), which will be held in a treasury investment account abroad.	All oil revenue is included in the budget since 2001 and the earlier practice of extra-budgetary expenditure financed by advances from the oil companies has been discontinued. However, the lack of transparency of transactions on the offshore treasury account continues.	Oil revenue to be used for investment purposes only.	Currently foreign assets are being accumulated; these are not in the form of long-term investments. However, the revised 2002 budget projects the creation of a special reserve fund (FFG).

14

Table 3 *(conlcuded)*

Country	Fiscal Rules	Integrity of Budget	Earmarking	Intergenerational Equity Provisions
Gabon	None.	All oil revenue is included in the budget.	None.	An FFG was created by law in 1998. According to the law, 10 percent of budgeted oil revenues as well as 50 percent of any windfall revenue are to be directed to the FFG. A first deposit of CFAF70 billion was made in 2002.
Nigeria	None.	Weaknesses in the fiscal administration of the oil sector may lead to inadequate allocation and collection of revenue for the government. Tax audits for the oil companies appear ineffective.	None.	None.

Sources: Country authorities; and IMF staff analyses.

Figure 4. Nigeria, Venezuela, and Indonesia: Fiscal Trends, 1978–2001

Oil Revenue

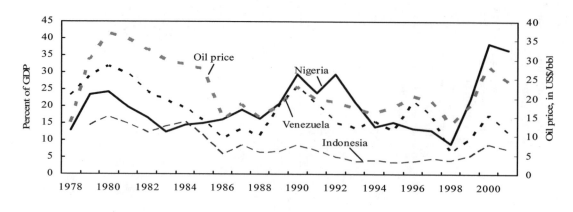

Total Expenditure

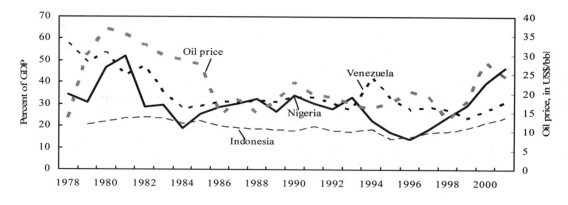

Overall Balance

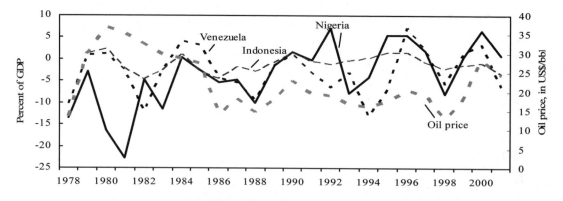

Source: Country authorities; and staff estimates.
Notes: Fiscal trends shown against left-hand axis, oil prices against right-hand axis.
      bbl = barrels of crude oil equivalent.

**Table 4. Correlation Between Oil Prices and
Government Spending, 1971–2001**

	Correlation Coefficient: Primary Expenditure versus	
	Current oil price	Oil price lagged by one period
Angola[1]	0.7	0.1
Cameroon	0.4	0.4
Republic of Congo[1]	0.3	0.5
Gabon	0.3	0.5
Nigeria	0.7	0.5

Sources: Country authorities; and IMF staff estimates.
[1]1989–2001.

Fiscal policy has generally not been successful in smoothing fluctuations in budgetary outlays in response to volatile oil prices. The correlation of fiscal expenditure and oil prices is high. Table 4 shows correlation coefficients of government primary expenditure and current oil prices (left column) and of government primary expenditure and oil prices lagged by one period (right column) for Angola, Cameroon, the Republic of Congo, Gabon, and Nigeria. The correlation coefficients are positive for all countries, and in Angola and Nigeria, they are larger for current than for lagged oil prices. In these countries, primary expenditure has been strongly correlated to current oil prices, as shown by a correlation coefficient of 0.7 (see also Figure 5 for the correlation between non-oil balances and oil prices).[11] Figure 6 shows overall and non-oil balances for the countries in the group between 1990 and 2001 (where data are available).

---

[11]These results should be interpreted with caution: while they give a sense of the cyclicality of fiscal spending, it is also important to keep in mind that price is but one key element. When a country has experienced large changes in oil production, a simple correlation between oil price and spending is likely to be a poor proxy for the correlation between government oil revenues and spending. Nevertheless, the table does convey the idea that government spending has been driven to an important extent by changes in current oil revenues in most countries.

Figure 5. Non-Oil Balances and Oil Prices, 1990–2002
(In percent of non-oil GDP, left scale, and in U.S. dollars per barrel, right scale)

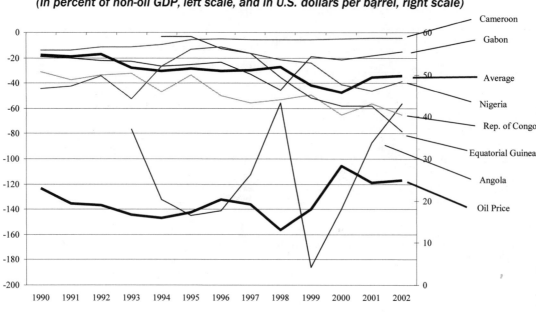

Sources: Country authorities; and IMF staff estimates.

In most countries, both public and private domestic demand components have been strongly correlated with oil revenue. As shown in Table 5 for the Republic of Congo and Gabon, the correlation between public expenditure and total oil export revenues (as a proxy for government oil revenues) is more pronounced in the Republic of Congo. (The correlation coefficient is 0.88, compared with 0.47 in Gabon.) Public demand in both countries is also strongly correlated with private demand, which means that public demand tends to reinforce, and possibly trigger, movements in private spending. Furthermore, the public sector has been a source of macroeconomic instability by virtue of its volatility—which has been twice that of private demand in both countries. (See also Chapter 6 on the correlation between oil prices and the REER).

Figure 6. Overall and Non-Oil Balances, 1990–2001

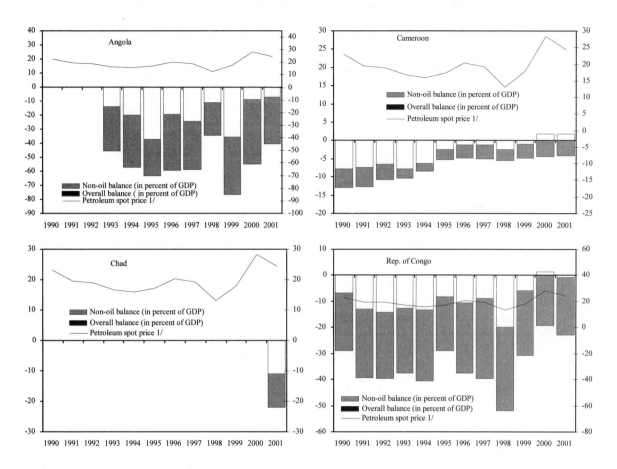

[1]Average U.K. Brent, Dubai, and West Texas Intermediate.

Figure 6 *(concluded)*

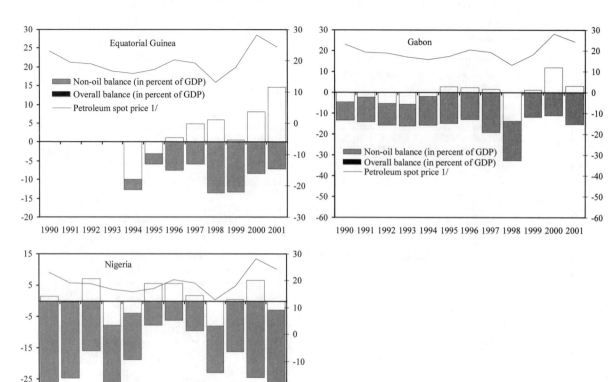

Sources: Country authorities; and IMF staff estimates.

[1]Average U.K. Brent, Dubai, and West Texas Intermediate.

Table 5. Oil Price Cyclicality of Public and Private Domestic Demand, 1990–2001

	Republic of Congo	Gabon
Correlation coefficient		
Oil export revenues, public demand	0.88	0.47
Oil export revenues, private demand	0.80	0.86
Public demand, private demand	0.69	0.63
Standard deviation		
Public demand growth	34	20
Private demand growth	17	11

Sources: Country authorities; and IMF staff estimates.

Governments do not make explicit provisions for the exhaustibility of oil revenue. In the Central African Economic and Monetary Community (CEMAC) countries, a legal framework to save part of oil revenues was put in place in 2001, but to date no country has made use of it. Two funds—one for short-term stabilization of oil receipts, the other for long-term savings for future generations—would be administered by the regional central bank. Chad is to adopt an explicit rule to deposit a part of oil revenue in a Fund for Future Generations (FFG). Gabon and Equatorial Guinea have created FFGs by laws that oblige the governments to deposit some specified amount of oil revenue as reserves in the regional central bank. Gabon made its first deposit, of some CFAF 70 billion, in the Bank of Central African States (BEAC) account in 2002.

Equatorial Guinea already has accumulated sizable deposits in offshore treasury accounts, but this is due more to a lack of administrative capacity to spend than to policy design. However, government spending has been rising rapidly during the last two years, and a continuation of the trend could threaten the authorities' ability to increase assets in the fund and ultimately lead to an unsustainable fiscal position.

C. Discussion and Recommendations

The IMF staff has consistently recommended fiscal restraint in African oil-producing countries in light of the revenue volatility and taking into account the limited absorptive capacity. It has also consistently recommended the integration of oil sector–related fiscal activities in the central government budget to enhance transparency and accountability, and progress has been achieved in this respect during the last few years.

Current practice in the African oil-producing countries presents a mixed picture. Some improvements in oil revenue management have been achieved, but much more needs to be done in order to ensure an adequate accounting for revenue and adoption of a rational fiscal policy stance. The fiscal stance in most countries has not fully reflected IMF advice; this is shown by the persistently high volatility of fiscal spending, the lack of diversification of government revenue sources, and the failure to accumulate foreign assets (and, in some countries, the accumulation of foreign debt).

Macroeconomic management can be improved by taking a medium- to long-term approach. Frequent adjustments of fiscal policy have detrimental economic effects. In the current environment of high oil prices, countries should be encouraged to make a serious effort to accumulate reserves. While the creation of savings funds large enough to ensure fiscal sustainability in the long run is probably not an option in countries such as Cameroon, Gabon, and Nigeria, even these countries need some reserves to cushion the blow of the next negative oil price shock. In this regard, greater emphasis should be given to the adoption of explicit fiscal rules.

Detailed discussions of intergenerational equity and the long-term sustainability of fiscal policy seem to have been held only in some countries. These should be important considerations to guide fiscal policy, in particular in oil-producing countries such as Equatorial Guinea and Chad, which have small populations but relatively large oil reserves. Given the limited administrative and, more generally, absorptive capacity, a rapid increase in fiscal expenditure in line with oil revenue would lead to large-scale economic disruptions. However, the size of the expected oil wealth relative to the non-oil economy means that, with an appropriately designed long-term policy, major sustainable improvements in living standards are possible even without high growth rates in the non-oil economy.

Participants at the Douala workshop broadly agreed that fiscal policy had not been well adapted to the challenges facing oil-exporting countries. In particular, they acknowledged the negative effects of oil revenue and fiscal spending volatility on their economies. They supported in principle the use of medium-term fiscal rules and stabilization funds to avoid the "boom-bust" cycles that have characterized many oil economies during the last 30 years.

Most participants insisted that the context of African countries had to be taken into account to determine a credible level of savings from oil revenue. They pointed out that the need to save could be difficult to accept for parts of civil society and the parliament, and that the expectations of the population had to be considered when deciding on the split among current spending, savings, and investment. Policies on savings and expenditure should not endanger political stability.

They further remarked that, in making decisions over domestic investments and savings, countries had to be able to assess domestic absorptive capacity and identify priorities for the use of public funds. Human resources in most SSA countries may not be sufficient to perform these functions well, and support from development partners may be needed.

4 Fiscal Policy Formulation

A. Background Discussion

While it may not be possible to identify an "optimal" fiscal policy for oil countries in general, the discussions in the previous section provide important issues for consideration by policymakers. In this section, we present some operational issues to help in the design of schemes for the use of oil revenue. This subsection presents (1) the case for a rule-based fiscal policy and (2) possible fiscal rules, including two "extremes" to be used as guideposts for the possible range of expenditure profiles.

Rule-based fiscal policy

The boom-bust cycles in oil-producing countries mentioned earlier have been at least partially caused by erratic fiscal policies that depended strongly on current oil price developments. Instead, a rule-based stabilization policy would have aimed at insulating the economy from the short-term volatility of oil prices and revenues. Such a rule-based fiscal policy would attempt to define a fiscal stance for a given, medium-term projection of oil prices and revenues. Budgets would be formulated within a medium-term framework. Oil price and revenue outturns would lead to changes in the net foreign assets position of the government. While fiscal policy rules by themselves may not necessarily guarantee stability, they do provide an anchor for policymakers and make it harder to pursue erratic policies in response to oil price shocks.

Government oil revenue and the expenditure it finances need to be integrated into the normal budgetary procedures. They then augment general government resources, as indicated by a larger overall fiscal surplus or deficit. Nevertheless, an operationally attractive tool for fiscal planners is the primary non-oil balance, defined as the overall balance of fiscal operations minus oil revenue and net interest income, and excluding foreign-financed investment.[12] The primary non-oil balance provides a useful indicator for measuring the direction and sustainability of fiscal policy. The overall fiscal balance depends strongly on developments in the oil sector, as its position will be comfortable when prices are (temporarily) high and provoke calls for fiscal retrenchment when prices are low. If only oil revenue is subtracted from the overall balance, the resulting non-oil balance reflects income from the net foreign assets of the government (debt service and interest on reserves). The use of the primary non-oil balance allows the targeting of a stable fiscal policy in line with general economic developments, and in most circumstances the primary non-oil balance will be negative to the extent that current oil revenue is used to finance expenditure. The primary non-oil balance makes apparent an increase in budgetary outlays in times of (temporarily) high oil prices, which can be difficult to reverse. In addition, this balance draws attention to the development of non-oil GDP and the associated taxable base. This focus on the non-oil economy supports the objective of diversifying the economy away from the oil sector.

A fiscal policy rule could be formulated on the basis of projected oil prices. In the budgeting process, that is, ex ante, a certain non-oil primary deficit would be targeted for the projected price, for example, US$20 per barrel, implying a certain overall budget balance; this balance would be positive if policymakers decided to aim to save part of the oil revenue. Any revenue above or below this reference price would increase or decrease the targeted stock of financial assets ex post, while leaving fiscal spending at the predetermined level. This price rule has obvious political advantages, as it is easily understood and the outcome is readily observable. Revenue changes stemming from factors other than international prices—for example, production increases due to new discoveries—could easily be built into any fiscal program.

The question is how to forecast oil prices during budgeting in order to draw up spending plans for projected oil revenue. As mentioned earlier, oil price developments can be described as a random walk. This means that frequent revisions of the oil price projections would be necessary. To underline the extent of the difficulties involved, we show in Figure 7 real oil prices over the last 40 years. (The U.S. GDP deflator is used to calculate real prices.) The very large swings in prices between the two oil crises (1973 and 1979) and the subsequent fall in prices in 1986 mask the considerable volatility during more "normal" times. Budgetary projections of oil revenue based on the average oil price of previous years were spectacularly wrong in a number of years. Use of the medium-term price-based rule therefore poses a dilemma: on the one hand, it demands that budgets be based on an oil price projection that remains fixed for

---

[12]This section draws heavily on Barnett and Ossowski (2002).

Figure 7. Oil Prices and Projections Based on Moving Averages, 1960–2002

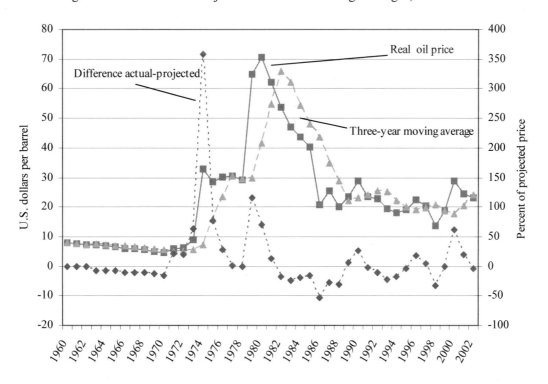

Sources: Country authorities; and IMF staff estimates.

some time; on the other hand, frequent revisions to the price projection may be necessary because of the large swings in oil prices observed in the past. Therefore, the risk of a prolonged oil price slump strengthens the case for using a fiscal rule with a pro-saving bias (the precautionary savings motive discussed in Section 3). Ideally, the country should first build up a cushion of reserves, and the price-based fiscal rule should be supplemented by a set of contingency measures that would be activated in exceptionally adverse circumstances.

Possible fiscal rules

Within this rule-based approach, a continuum of possibilities exists for the choice of fiscal stance at given oil prices. Two "extreme" solutions frame the range of options, while a third lies in between. The first extreme option is that policymakers prepare a budget that is designed to spend all projected oil revenue, with no saving foreseen. The second extreme alternative is that policymakers decide to save all current oil revenue and spend only the real projected return on assets accumulated in previous years; that is, they cautiously think that "a bird in the hand is worth two in the bush" in the highly uncertain world of the oil market. The third, more moderate option may appeal most to the theory purists: set the level of fiscal spending equal to permanent per capita income. We present the three options in order of the fiscal spending they imply—the first extreme option, the moderate option, and the second extreme option—and give numerical examples.

Going on a binge

Under the first extreme option, which we call "going on a binge," a country would adopt a rule that calls for balanced budgets over the next three to five years at the given oil revenue projection. To balance the budget, the overall balance is targeted at zero, the non-oil balance is negative by the amount of oil revenue, and the primary non-oil balance differs from the non-oil balance by the amount of net income from foreign assets (or debt service). This may be the best option for countries like Cameroon, where there is a significant non-oil economy, oil revenue–financed spending has become entrenched, and oil production is stable or declining.

Purist

Oil receipts can be regarded as the proceeds from the sale of a natural asset, rather than as current revenue. Under the moderate option, which we call the "purist" option, fiscal policy should aim at preserving the government's net worth, which is the net present value of future flows of revenues and debt payments. In order to maintain net worth and to safeguard fiscal sustainability, it is necessary to build income-generating assets from oil revenue or reduce outstanding debt, instead of using it to finance current expenditure.

One way of operationalizing the sustainability requirement based on net worth is by calculating permanent (annual) income from oil reserves. This is the maximum amount that can be treated as current revenue each year—hence, the amount that could be used to finance public spending. In principle, permanent income can be calculated by summing up the estimated government revenue from oil production over the lifetime of the reserves, appropriately discounted to arrive at the present value of oil reserves, and then calculating a permanent income stream that would represent the same net present value. A country's fiscal policy would be considered sustainable provided its non-oil fiscal deficits did not exceed its permanent oil income.

Figure 8. Alternative Fiscal Rules, 2002–25

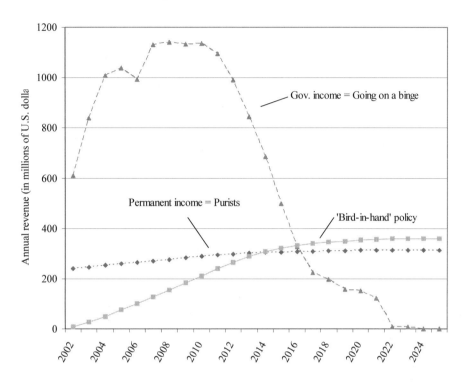

Sources: Country authorities; and IMF staff estimates.

To illustrate the concepts, we present below data for government oil revenue from a small number of oil fields in the early years of development (similar to the existing oil sector in Equatorial Guinea). Figure 8 compares the three fiscal policy rules discussed here. The first series, "going on a binge," shows current government revenue based on standard production-sharing contracts and World Economic Outlook (WEO) oil price projections.[13] Oil revenue in 2002 reaches around $600 million. The figure shows the fast rise of revenue to more than $1,100 million in 2011 and the decline that will result if no major new discoveries are made, with abandonment of the last remaining well in 2025. The first policy option described above would aim to predict revenue each year and spend it. For a small country such as Equatorial Guinea, this is a binge indeed, as spending in the peak revenue year would equal about $1,500 per capita.

---

[13]WEO projections reach only until 2007. From then on, prices are assumed to increase by 2 percent a year.

The second series shows budgetary spending based on the permanent income equivalent of the net present value of future oil revenue (constant in per capita terms under the assumption that population grows by 2.5 percent per year initially and stabilizes around 2020). This is the "purist" option. If the net present value of future oil revenue were put into an investment account in 2002, the interest from the deposit would allow fiscal spending starting at $230 million in 2002, which would then rise before stabilizing at more than $300 million. The permanent income equivalent of government revenue projected from current proven reserves is about $530 per capita. However, as discussed earlier, changes in the reserve estimates, the price projections, or the assumed rate of return on the portfolio would change the permanent income equivalent.

Bird in hand

The second "extreme" option for a fiscal policy rule, the "bird-in-hand" approach, describes a cautionary fiscal policy aimed at building income-generating assets and limiting consumption to the income actually generated. The amount of revenue available for consumption purposes the following year would be determined as the projected return on assets accumulated in an FFG by the end of the current year.[14] The overall balance would be highly positive during most of the lifetime of oil reserves, the non-oil balance would be targeted at zero, and the primary non-oil balance would be negative by the projected amount of net income from foreign assets (i.e., interest on assets accumulated in the FFG in previous years minus debt service). If assets are held in a well-diversified portfolio, returns will be much less volatile than the oil price. In addition, this fiscal rule does not require long-term projections based on "heroic" assumptions.

The third series in Figure 8 shows this "bird-in-hand" alternative. It assumes that oil revenue of about $600 million is paid into the FFG in 2002. Interest earnings rise fast with the buildup of deposits in the FFG until they stabilize at about $380 million at the end of the oil era. The growth rate of interest earnings reaches 20 percent per year on average during the first ten years; interest income grows to about $100 million in the first five years. If this rise in income were matched by a rise in fiscal expenditure, spending would probably overwhelm the country's absorptive capacity during the first decade.[15]

---

[14]This is the fiscal rule followed by Norway (see Box 1).

[15]Actual spending in the 2002 budget is $140 million.

Box 1. Fiscal Policy in Natural Resource–Based Countries

Diamonds and fiscal policy in Botswana

Fiscal surpluses enabled the government to accumulate large balances with the Bank of Botswana. The revenues from the mineral sector consist of a royalty (10 percent of gross sales), company income tax (25 percent of profits), and dividends. These revenues have been earmarked for development purposes, while recurrent expenditures are financed from revenues not related to the diamond industry. In addition, the income from foreign assets has enabled Botswana to cope adequately with internal economic shocks during 2001–02: a cyclical downturn in the diamond market; a large depreciation of the South African rand, which weakened the competitiveness of Botswana's manufacturing sector; unusual weather conditions; and a regional food shortage.

Oil and fiscal policy in Kuwait

In 1960, the authorities created the General Reserve Fund (GRF), financed by rising budget surpluses; no accumulation rules for the GRF were defined. In 1976, formalizing the policy of reserve accumulation, the authorities established the Reserve Fund for Future Generations (RFFG) with the objective of providing a stream of income once oil production declined. The RFFG consisted initially of half of the GRF's resources, augmented annually with 10 percent of total (oil and non-oil) revenues. On the whole, these funds have been supported by relatively prudent fiscal policies— conservative oil price assumptions and a restraint on expenditures. Almost all of the RFFG assets are held abroad.

Oil and fiscal policy in Norway

Norway has been able to enjoy substantial fiscal surpluses with the rise of its oil production and exports since 1975. The oil wealth is managed through the State Petroleum Fund (SPF) established in 1990. The purpose is to preserve national wealth for future generations in sufficient amounts for each individual to inherit at least as large an amount as that of the present generation. All of the government's net income from oil is fed into the SPF, from which an annual transfer is made to the treasury to meet the non-oil deficit in the budget. The non-oil deficit is limited by law to the projected income from the assets in the SPF.

Other oil-producing areas

Alaska deposits 25 percent of oil revenue in savings funds irrespective of oil market developments, and the assets in the fund can be used only following a change to the constitution voted by the Alaskan population. Kazakhstan deposits revenue in excess of the budget reference price into the mineral fund; revenue shortfalls are compensated by transfers from the fund. Oman also has rules in place to deposit oil revenue in excess of the reference price into different funds, but recently has not always followed the rules and has accumulated little. Azerbaijan set up a savings fund to receive revenue from new oil fields, which are expected to increase massively over the next few years. Venezuela has had a mixed experience with its stabilization fund. The initial rules established that oil revenue above the threshold price should be deposited in the fund. However, as the central government remained in deficit in 1999 and 2000 despite the recovery in oil prices, it could only make deposits into the fund with recourse to other financing.

This "bird-in-hand" option is a solution to the problem posed by uncertainties in the determination of permanent income.[16] Following this rule will (1) raise fiscal expenditure relatively slowly at the beginning of oil production, thus providing time for an increase in absorptive capacity; (2) increase fiscal expenditure continuously until the end of oil production, which is politically easier to accomplish than to hold expenditure constant at the assumed permanent income level; (3) provide the most dependable stabilization of fiscal policy, since the spending planned for the current year is always in line with projected non-oil revenue (including interest on foreign assets); and (4) lead to a rapid buildup of assets, so that even a very large underperformance of the oil sector—whether because of catastrophic events or structural shifts in the oil market (e.g., the obsolescence of oil)—will not force the government into retrenchment. Volatility and costly downward adjustments to fiscal expenditure will be avoided. This rule is particularly attractive to new, small oil-producing countries, where oil revenue is rising rapidly and threatens to overwhelm the non-oil economy. However, political acceptance may be difficult to achieve, in particular in the early years of oil development, when the need for public spending is perceived to be large and the prospects for rising oil revenue in the future are clear. For small countries, it is also possible that interest income may rise more rapidly than absorptive capacity, and that expenditure would be held below interest income.

B. Current Practice

Government budgets are usually based on projected oil prices and production volumes, and contingencies are generally not taken into account. It is often not clear which source of oil price projections is used. Oil revenue is usually deposited in the central banks, and oil revenue constitutes part of general government resources in most countries.[17] Oil revenues are now generally included in the budget, and budgets give a good picture of the expected financial operations of the government. In Angola, Sonangol, the state oil company, retains 10 percent of oil profits to cover the costs that it incurs as a regulator on behalf of the state, and some bonuses are paid directly to various autonomous social funds with unclear legal bases. A high level of cross arrears exists between the Angolan Treasury and Sonangol. In Equatorial Guinea, oil revenue has been included in the budget only since 2001, and a degree of realism and accuracy in budget projections was achieved only when the revised budget for 2002 was submitted to parliament in May 2002. In Nigeria, set percentages of government oil revenue are transferred to provincial governments, whereas the other

---

[16]The expression was first used in this context by Bjerkholt (2002). See Barnett and Ossowski (2002).

[17]Exceptions are Angola, where the Ministry of Finance and Sonangol recently moved deposits to private banks, and Equatorial Guinea, where oil companies pay government revenue in bank accounts abroad and fiscal surpluses remain in these bank accounts.

countries have centralized budgets. Under the Law on Petroleum Revenue Management, Chad's oil revenue is to be included in the budget.

Regarding expenditures financed by government oil revenue, Chad and Equatorial Guinea have adopted rules that limit the use of such revenue. Equatorial Guinea restricts the use of oil revenue to public investment only, whereas in Chad oil revenue is to be used mostly for earmarked social sector spending. In Cameroon, part of any windfall revenue is to be spent in the social sectors and part for reducing domestic debt arrears. In the Republic of Congo, a large portion of fiscal oil revenue (about 40 percent in 2001) is precommitted for the service of collateralized debt and some investment projects.

C. Discussion and Recommendations

Participants in the Douala workshop acknowledged the importance of rules for guiding the formulation of fiscal policy, so as to limit the negative impact of oil revenue volatility and to ensure transparency and credibility. They also broadly agreed on the relevance of the use of both the price-based rule and the non-oil budget balance as tools for formulating and monitoring fiscal policy, although some voiced skepticism as to the usefulness of the non-oil balance in view of the low share in GDP of the non-oil sectors in most of the countries concerned.

It is much more difficult to make the case for accumulating savings for future generations in the form of foreign financial assets. Participants argued that physical investment might be just as useful to ensure future growth, while acknowledging that absorptive capacity may be limited and some temporary financial savings therefore justified.

It will be important to raise absorptive capacity, which would allow for an increase in the effective use of oil revenue. It would be difficult to save oil windfalls in the face of pressing needs to build countries' physical infrastructure and human capital. African policymakers feel that any decision on savings and expenditure should ensure political stability, and that certain institutional characteristics, such as fiscal federalism, might be associated with higher spending pressures.

There is a growing need to deepen the dialogue with civil society, and particularly parliaments, on fiscal policy options. Oil revenue management priorities should become part of stakeholder discussions as spending priorities already are in countries that are preparing poverty reduction strategy papers (PRSPs).

5 Persistent Surpluses and Accumulation of Assets

Background Discussion

We have presented the rationale for saving at least some of the current oil revenue. The question remains whether savings should be used for (1) repayment of existing government debt, (2) investment in domestic assets, or (3) investment in external assets. In some countries, debt service on existing concessional debt can be below the returns that would be achieved by investing reserves in a well-constructed international portfolio. Saving part of the oil revenue stream can, therefore, generate income-earning assets whose flows can be more than sufficient to cover existing debt-service payments. Prudence would advise against borrowing in anticipation of higher oil revenue in the future, and this includes borrowing when oil prices are thought to be temporarily below their medium-term average. Leaving aside the danger that higher oil revenue may fail to materialize, a high sovereign risk premium in oil countries in Africa can make borrowing very expensive.

Domestic investment opportunities in most African countries are limited by the small capitalization or nonexistence of capital markets and by capacity constraints. In addition, investment in physical assets has to be limited to safeguard the macroeconomic stability and competitiveness of the non-oil economy, and, therefore, part of the oil revenue would have to be sterilized. Some of the savings would thus best be invested in financial assets abroad.

It is important that all oil-related financial operations be included in the government budget and that savings funds be created as an integral part of the budgetary operations. Savings funds can be set up so that they will automatically stabilize fiscal policy as assets are accumulated according to the actual fiscal surplus achieved at the end of the fiscal year. In contrast, many countries in the past implemented allocation rules requiring, for example, that a certain percentage of oil revenue be paid into the fund. Applying this allocation rule independent of the overall fiscal position of the government can—and has in several countries (for example, Venezuela)—lead to the simultaneous accumulation of assets in the fund and government borrowing to finance an overall deficit. To avoid this paradoxical situation, savings should be determined as a residual, and the fiscal policy stance should be appropriate to produce the desired level of the overall deficit and accumulation of assets. However, in order to protect wealth on a long-term basis, legal barriers against withdrawing from a fund would probably be helpful—for example, a constitutional requirement that budgets cannot be based on withdrawals from the fund and that such withdrawals can be made only under emergency conditions and if authorized by parliament (as is the case in Kuwait and Alaska). In implementing the budget, if revenue shortfalls were to occur due to lower-than-expected oil prices or unforeseen events in the oil sector, the fund should be allowed to stabilize public spending—for example, through a supplementary budget approved by parliament.

Regarding institutional aspects, the transformation of government savings into foreign assets is a question of reserve management. Traditionally, this has been the prerogative of the central bank, and a case can be made for retaining a strong role for the central bank in the management of these oil savings. In practical terms, all oil revenue could be credited to a special treasury account at the central bank. Debits from the special treasury account would then finance the non-oil deficit, and the central bank, together with an oversight committee and, probably, some external financial experts, would determine how to invest government savings abroad.

B. Current Practice

All the countries channel at least part of their fiscal surpluses from oil revenue (insofar as surpluses exist) into treasury accounts with their central banks. Equatorial Guinea holds large deposits in a bank account abroad, in addition to contributing to reserves at the BEAC (see Table 6). The foreign bank account is not transparent; access to the account is restricted to the president. The rules of the BEAC do not allow the holding of such external deposits. Angola has reported large fiscal deficits over the last five years, and foreign exchange reserves at the central bank are low.

Table 6. Current Practice in Foreign Reserve and Debt Management

Country	Reserves in the Central Bank	Borrowing Against Oil Revenue
Angola	Trends in government deposits at the central bank have mirrored trends in oil exports.	Yes. Borrowing terms are not transparent.
Cameroon	All foreign exchange earnings mandatorily repatriated to the BEAC. Oil revenue in excess of programmed level is deposited in CFA francs in a treasury account at the BEAC to be used for priority infrastructure and social expenditure and to reduce domestic arrears.	None.
Chad	Law creating a Fund for Future Generations stipulates that assets be held with an international financial institution and invested in long-term instruments. This is inconsistent with BEAC rules.	None.
Republic of Congo	Reserves are held in the BEAC.	Extensive use of oil-collateralized borrowing from foreign commercial banks.
Equatorial Guinea	Government holds foreign exchange deposits abroad and makes contributions to reserves of the BEAC. Information on transactions on the offshore bank account lacking.	The government has been borrowing from oil companies against future oil revenue but extent and terms of such borrowing not transparent.
Gabon	Contribution to BEAC reserves declined sharply in 2001.	Gabon has never collateralized debt with oil revenue. However, the boom and bust of the international oil market were reflected in the budget's borrowing needs. Borrowing was generally carried out on unfavorable commercial terms. There are indications that the frequent resort to advances from oil companies has been discontinued.
Nigeria	Account for the management of fiscal surplus does not exist. However, higher-than-budgeted oil revenues are set aside in a so-called excess proceeds account which are part of foreign exchange reserves. These accounts are drawn down on the basis of discretionary decisions by the executive.	Debt is not collateralized with oil revenue. However, the "ratchet effect" has led to accumulation of large debt both in years of low and high oil prices.

Sources: Country authorities; and IMF staff analyses.

34

In Cameroon and Nigeria, deposits in central banks serve in principle as instruments to stabilize the budget. In Chad and Equatorial Guinea, FFGs have been set up, which accordingly will not be available to finance government operations until oil revenues decline. Chad's FFG is to be managed by an international financial institution and invested in long-term financial assets. Under the staff-monitored program, the Congolese authorities have set up a special treasury account at the central bank to deposit excess oil revenue but have so far not made use of it. In contrast, despite higher-than-projected oil revenue, the government's net indebtedness to the central bank has continued to grow, reaching the limit set under BEAC policy. The Republic of Congo and Gabon have seen their contribution to BEAC foreign reserves diminish significantly in recent years.

C. Discussion and Recommendations

Participants acknowledged the trade-offs between, on the one hand, investing in financial assets or repaying debt and, on the other, investing in infrastructure and human development—including the political difficulties involved in generating a social consensus on the need to save oil revenues. As mentioned above, the need to accumulate financial assets for stabilization purposes is recognized, as is the need for investment in infrastructure and human development that would transfer wealth to future generations. Participants therefore viewed the financial savings option with some skepticism. They nevertheless acknowledged the constraints placed by poor institutional capacity on the identification and execution of high-quality projects. The strategy of saving on a temporary basis to accommodate absorptive capacity constraints was more easily accepted.

It will be important to continue the discussions on long-term sustainability and intergenerational equity issues. Depending on country circumstances, savings for future generations are in order, in particular in small countries with limited reserve outlooks and high oil revenue dependency. Even in cases where domestic absorptive capacity can be expanded sufficiently and government investment has demonstrably high rates of return, policymakers still have to discuss foreign exchange availability when the oil runs out, and they may come to the conclusion that some international savings are needed.

6 Exchange Rate Regimes and Competitiveness

Background Discussion

Oil-exporting countries have used a variety of exchange rate arrangements, as shown in Figure 9. At the end of 2001, about 18 of the 29 oil-producing IMF member countries (excluding the former Soviet bloc countries) used some form of fixed exchange rate regime, while 11 opted for either managed or independent floating. This suggests that, in practice, the choice of an exchange rate arrangement is not a straightforward exercise; instead, exchange rate policy has to be based on country-specific considerations, including the relative openness of the economy, in terms of both current and capital accounts, and the relative prevalence of real or nominal shocks. Exchange rate policy will also have to take into account the monetary policy and institutional framework in which it is set.[18] This subsection describes first general considerations, then potential advantages of flexible exchange rates, and finally policies in support of fixed exchange rates.

General considerations

Exchange rate policy has an important role to play within a macroeconomic policy framework and can contribute to the maintenance of macroeconomic stability. For an oil-exporting country, the risk to macroeconomic stability comes mainly from changes in the international oil price, which lead to export revenue changes. These changes, unless accompanied by changes in foreign and domestic savings, result in balance of payments disequilibria that can be corrected only via

---

[18]For a recent reminder, see, for example, Laidler (1999), who uses the term *monetary order* to describe the set of arrangements comprising monetary policy, along with the framework of institutions, goals, and beliefs in which this policy is conducted.

Figure 9. Oil-Producing Developing Countries: Exchange Rate Regimes, 2001

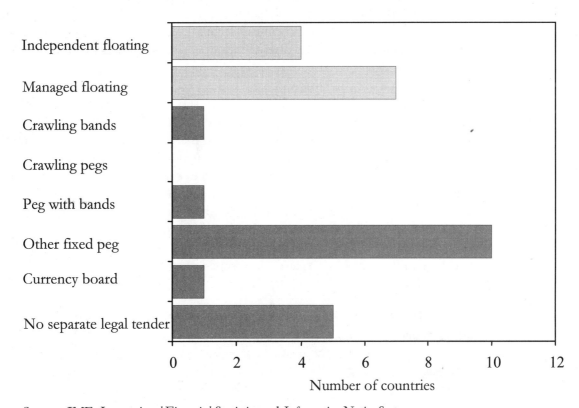

Source: IMF, *International Financial Statistics* and *Information Notice System*.

real exchange rate adjustment. This adjustment, or the change in the relative price of tradables and nontradables, will take place regardless of the nominal exchange rate regime in place; however, the exchange rate regime determines whether adjustment will be preceded by a change in the nominal exchange rate or a change in the domestic price level.

An increase in the price of oil leads to higher private and public oil revenue, usually received in U.S. dollars. The conversion of this dollar inflow into domestic currency puts pressure on the currency to appreciate. Policymakers are facing a dilemma: they can either let the nominal exchange rate appreciate, or the central bank can buy up foreign exchange and increase foreign reserves in order to avoid a nominal appreciation (as in a fixed exchange rate regime). However, this latter option creates excess liquidity in the economy, which, since sterilization efforts cannot be sustained for a long period (and the accompanying high domestic interest rates may be undesirable), would in turn lead to higher domestic spending and inflation.

A nominal appreciation means that consumers will find imported goods cheaper than goods produced at home, and producers will find it more profitable to produce for the domestic market than for export; as a result, the competitiveness of the non-oil tradable sector declines. Higher imports and lower non-oil exports close the balance of payments disequilibrium created by increased oil export earnings. In a fixed exchange rate regime, domestic inflation leads to a similar adjustment. A traditional three-goods model—oil, a tradable good (say, manufacturing), and a nontradable good (say, services)—can provide useful insights into how this comes about. Higher domestic spending from excess liquidity raises the price of services relative to manufacturing because the supply of manufactured goods can be expanded through imports (at prevailing international prices), whereas additional services can be produced only with the existing scarce domestic production factors. The increase in the price of services encourages the movement of factors of production away from manufacturing, with employers in the service sector bidding up wages in order to attract additional labor. In a new equilibrium, the output of services will be higher, and that of manufacturing lower, and the competitiveness of the non-oil tradable sector will have declined.

The predicted result of real exchange rate appreciation in response to an improvement in the terms of trade is not affected by the existing exchange rate regime. The essential element of the economy's adjustment relates to the *relative price change* (services versus manufacturing) that takes place regardless of the regime.[19] Yet the exchange rate regime itself will influence how the adjustment in relative prices is brought about—an important consideration in weighing the relative merits of alternative exchange rate regimes.

Potential advantages of the flexible exchange rate regime

A flexible exchange rate regime offers potential advantages to a resource-dependent country: it can facilitate the economy's adjustment to terms-of-trade changes and help maintain macroeconomic stability. However, in practice, these potential advantages can be undermined by poorly designed or poorly implemented monetary and fiscal policies—a frequent occurrence in countries with weak institutions, low central bank credibility, and persistent fiscal pressures. A flexible exchange rate regime facilitates a relative price adjustment while allowing monetary policy to be geared toward controlling domestic inflation. Consider, in particular, a long-lasting or permanent oil price decline. Under such a scenario, the country's real exchange rate will depreciate. Whereas

---

[19]The decline in manufacturing in response to this price change is a phenomenon commonly called the Dutch disease (see Section 3). This is an unfortunate term because it gives an undeserved negative connotation to a resource allocation process that is economically quite rational and that, in and of itself, does not imply a decrease in the country's overall GDP.

in a flexible exchange rate regime this adjustment can be achieved through a nominal exchange rate depreciation, under a fixed rate regime this requires a decline in domestic money wages and prices.[20] In an economy with sticky wages and prices, the adjustment process may involve periods of unemployment and output losses.

Thus, in general, we would expect oil-exporting countries with flexible exchange rate regimes to enjoy greater output and price stability than countries with fixed rates. However, this relative advantage will be realized only if it is set within a coherent monetary policy framework, ideally supported also by a sound fiscal policy. Under a lax monetary policy, a nominal depreciation may trigger an inflationary spiral, which will tend to frustrate the necessary adjustment in relative prices. In those conditions, the process of adjustment may be just as drawn out and difficult as under the fixed exchange rate.

Policies in support of a fixed exchange rate regime

Maintenance of a fixed exchange rate constrains the country's monetary policy and may render adjustment to terms-of-trade changes more difficult. On the upside, such an arrangement, if set within a coherent monetary framework supported by strong institutional safeguards, can provide much-needed policy credibility and contribute to greater overall macroeconomic stability. A sound fiscal policy is particularly critical to ensuring the ongoing viability of a fixed exchange rate regime. In addition, structural policies aimed at enhancing the flexibility of goods and factor markets and creating an environment conducive to private sector development are important in facilitating the economy's adjustment to permanent changes in the terms of trade.

Fiscal policy assumes an important role in macroeconomic stabilization under a fixed exchange rate regime. A potentially negative effect on the domestic economy from international oil price swings can be attenuated by a fiscal policy that is actively geared toward stabilizing domestic demand.[21] Establishing a stable fiscal spending pattern is important for maintenance of macroeconomic stability when dealing with year-to-year swings in the terms of trade. However, in a scenario in which international oil prices or domestic oil production are on a long-term decline, maintaining fiscal spending at levels established in "good" times poses risks to fiscal sustainability and delays the needed adjustment in the

---

[20]Reinhart and Rogoff (2002) find that, between 1971 and 2001, the CFA franc zone countries—commodity exporters with a hard exchange rate peg—experienced more frequent episodes of deflation than other countries.

[21]In sub-Saharan Africa, most of the income generated in the oil sector is shared by foreign oil companies and the domestic public sector. With the repatriation of the foreign portion of the income, the risk to domestic stability comes largely from procyclical fiscal expenditures. In these circumstances, fiscal policy needs to aim at stabilizing public expenditures.

economy. In that case, the adjustment needs to be driven by the supply side of the economy—flexible goods and factor markets can ease the adjustment necessary to reallocate production from services toward manufacturing. Under a fixed exchange rate regime, pursuit of structural policies aimed at enhancing the flexibility and resilience of the non-oil economy is essential.[22]

B. Current Practice

In the group of SSA oil exporters, five countries—Cameroon, Chad, the Republic of Congo, Equatorial Guinea, and Gabon—are members, along with the Central African Republic, of CEMAC. They share a common currency, the CFA franc, which had been pegged to the French franc and, since the beginning of 1999, has been pegged to the euro. The exchange rate regimes of the other two oil exporters—Angola and Nigeria—are classified as a managed float.

CEMAC countries

CEMAC countries belong to a monetary union—the Union Monétaire de l'Afrique Centrale (UMAC)—in which the responsibility for monetary policy has been delegated to the regional central bank (BEAC).[23] CEMAC's monetary arrangement leaves little scope for an independent monetary policy even at the regional level—it is essentially a rule-based system characterized by the peg to the euro, convertibility, limits on central bank lending to governments, and minimum legal levels of foreign reserves (Boxes 2 and 3). Any decision to realign the common currency has to be made jointly, which rules out unilateral actions by individual members for reasons of political expediency. Between 1971 and 2001, CEMAC oil producers' GDP per capita growth averaged 2.4 percent, compared with a 0.9 percent average for all oil producers (Table 7). Inflation performance was also better for CEMAC oil producers: 8.4 percent versus 26.6 percent for the whole group. The record is less clear cut in terms of inflation variability as the average variability was lower for CEMAC oil producers (11.6) than for the group as a whole (47.8); however, the median value is slightly higher for CEMAC (9.4 versus 7.8 for the group as a whole).

---

[22]This will be even more important in countries where the oil sector has some interaction in domestic factor markets.

[23]According to its statutes (Article 1) ". . . the Bank issues the currency of the Union and guarantees its stability. Without undermining this objective, the bank provides support to the economic policies within the Union. The mission of the Bank is to define and conduct the monetary policy for the countries of the Union; to buy and sell foreign currency; to hold and manage the exchange reserves of member countries; to ensure smooth functioning of the payments system of the Union."

> ### Box 2. Oil Funds and Foreign Exchange Management in CEMAC Countries
>
> In 2001, the BEAC (the common central bank of the Central African Economic and Monetary Community (CEMAC) countries) created a framework for two funds: one to help achieve the short-term stabilization of oil receipts and the other to accumulate long-term savings for future generations. Countries can pay 50 percent of their "excess" oil receipts into the *stabilization fund*—excess defined as revenue corresponding to the oil price exceeding its five-year average. Conversely, countries can make drawings from the fund corresponding to 50 percent of the shortfall. A country's net balance in the stabilization fund must remain positive. Up to 10 percent of oil revenues can be deposited in the *savings fund*. To date, no country has made a deposit in either fund—an outcome that seems to reflect unresolved issues relating to the management of the funds and the types of assets that the funds could hold, as well as concern about low rates of return offered by the BEAC.
>
> The rules of the monetary union stipulate that foreign assets be kept partly with the BEAC (35 percent) and partly in the BEAC's operations account with the French Treasury. As foreign exchange reserves, these funds would need to be held in short-term liquid assets. Thus, at the moment, it is not clear how, under the current rules, long-term investment objectives of the savings fund—including the possibility of holding longer-term, higher-return-yielding assets, including equities and bonds—can be reconciled with the pooling of reserves. Furthermore, the requirement to pool reserves seems to rule out a separate investment of foreign exchange owned by a country's fund for future generations.

The greatest risk to the stability and continued viability of the CFA franc peg comes from weak fiscal policy and, in the case of oil exporters, from procyclical fiscal policy, in particular. Part of the risk stems from the rules themselves—for example, linking the government's credit ceiling at the central bank to its fiscal revenues effectively means that when oil prices are relatively high—and so, presumably, is government revenue—the government will be able to borrow more from the central bank. This occurred in the second half of the 1970s, when the CEMAC countries benefited from the increases in their terms of trade while at the same time allowing their outstanding borrowing from the BEAC to rise.

In recent years, with relatively favorable international oil prices, excess demand pressures stemming from expansionary fiscal spending have been a concern in most CEMAC countries, despite the fact that no oil producer except Chad has been in violation of the convergence criterion for the basic fiscal balance

Box 3. CEMAC Monetary Arrangement

The arrangement is underpinned by the following elements:

- Convertibility of the CFA franc is guaranteed by the French Treasury.
- Transfers are free within the zone.
- Foreign exchange reserves are centralized at two levels: at the regional central bank (the BEAC), and at the French Treasury. Member countries have to maintain at least 65 percent of their foreign exchange reserves in the operations account of the French Treasury.

The BEAC's overriding policy objective is to maintain the stability of the common currency, with a subordinate objective of providing support to the economic policies within the union. There is little scope for independent monetary policy—the maintenance of the peg to the euro means that the monetary policy stance in the region is essentially determined by the actions of the European Central Bank.

Monetary policy is supported through a number of safeguards. Lending by the BEAC to central governments is capped at 20 percent of government fiscal receipts collected in the preceding year.[1] The BEAC is required to maintain 20 percent foreign exchange cover of its sight liabilities, a limit designed to act in practice as a barrier against open-ended access to the operations account that the bank maintains with the French Treasury. Corrective measures—increase in interest rates and reduction in the refinancing of commercial banks—are envisaged should the floor be breached for three consecutive months.

To ensure consistency between its monetary policy and national economic and fiscal policies, the BEAC conducts an annual financial programming exercise, designed to set specific targets of credit for each government consistent with a target level of net domestic assets and gross foreign assets of the BEAC. The programming exercise is complemented by an annual macroeconomic surveillance exercise, which is part of an agenda of intensified regional surveillance and integration. In the surveillance exercise, CEMAC's Executive Secretariat evaluates the member countries' policies relative to the following targets: nonnegative basic balance; a level of domestic and foreign debt not exceeding 70 percent of GDP; nonaccumulation of domestic and external arrears; and annual inflation of no more than 3 percent.

---

[1]This rule will cease to be in effect on January 1, 2004, with the planned elimination of the BEAC's monetary financing of government deficits, which will be phased in over ten years.

(nonnegative) since 1999. In 2001, the inflation convergence criterion of 3 percent was breached by Equatorial Guinea (12.0 percent) and Chad (12.4 percent). The net foreign position of the CEMAC as a whole deteriorated as well, with net foreign assets declining from CFAF 274 billion to CFAF 133 billion in that year.

Table 7. Economic Performance of Oil Exporters, 1971–2001[1]

| | Total | Peggers | | Floaters | | |
		All	CEMAC	All	Angola	Nigeria
GDP per capita growth, period annual average, percent						
Average						
1971–2001	0.9	1.0	2.4	0.9	-1.8	0.7
1971–81	1.1	1.3	2.0	0.9	-3.7	-1.2
1981–91	-0.6	-1.6	0.1	0.6	0.5	2.9
1991–2001	2.0	3.0	5.2	0.9	-1.9	0.0
Median						
1971–2001	0.7	1.0	1.0	0.7	-1.8	0.7
1971–81	1.6	2.7	3.2	1.2	-3.7	-1.2
1981–91	0.1	-0.1	0.5	0.4	0.5	2.9
1991–2001	1.0	1.6	0.0	0.5	-1.9	0.0
Inflation, period annual average, percent						
Average						
1971–2001	26.6	9.5	8.4	49.5	356.2	22.0
1971–81	13.2	11.1	10.3	16.0	40.1	15.8
1981–91	19.1	9.6	7.9	31.8	10.1	19.7
1991–2001	49.0	7.6	6.8	104.2	1050.1	31.2
Median						
1971–2001	10.5	7.3	7.5	21.7	356.2	22.0
1971–81	12.1	11.0	10.7	14.5	40.1	15.8
1981–91	9.2	4.5	5.8	14.9	10.1	19.7
1991–2001	7.9	4.4	6.8	15.9	1050.1	31.2
Deviation of inflation rate						
Average						
1971–2001	47.8	8.6	11.6	100.1	940.4	18.8
1971–81	13.6	7.5	10.0	21.8	38.1	10.4
1981–91	65.0	7.7	12.5	141.5	1419.4	22.5
1991–2001	7.6	3.8	3.0	12.7	86.5	5.1
Median						
1971–2001	7.8	6.8	9.4	14.5	940.0	18.8
1971–81	5.7	6.3	4.8	5.4	38.1	10.4
1981–91	7.4	5.1	13.0	16.4	1419.4	22.5
1991–2001	2.7	1.7	2.7	4.8	86.5	5.1

[1]A group comprising 38 oil-producing developing countries.

Angola and Nigeria

Viewed over the longer 1971–2001 period, the economic performance of Angola and Nigeria was inferior to that of the CEMAC countries (Table 7). Annual per capita GDP growth averaged –1.8 percent for Angola and 0.7 percent for Nigeria; inflation 356 percent and 22 percent, respectively; and the standard deviation of inflation 940 percent and 19 percent, respectively.

An expansionary fiscal policy bias and fiscal dominance have tended to complicate the conduct of monetary policy and reduce the effectiveness of the exchange rate as a policy instrument in both countries. Monetary conditions have been considerably unsettled in Angola, which experienced an average inflation rate in excess of 1,000 percent in 1991–2001. Nigeria fared better, with inflation averaging 31.2 percent between 1991 and 2001. However, in this period, the central bank faced difficulties in meeting its monetary and inflation objectives. Its monetary policy was generally accommodative of expansionary fiscal policies and demand pressures. As a result, liquidity exceeded targeted levels, and base and broad money objectives were persistently breached.

Although the exchange rate regimes of the two countries are classified as floating, the authorities in both countries have often attempted to manage their exchange rates. In Angola, the official intervention in 2001 reflected a policy of de facto exchange rate–based stabilization. In Nigeria, past attempts to tightly manage the exchange rate were reflected in sharp changes in international reserves and the widening premium in the parallel exchange rate.

Parallel foreign exchange rate markets have been active in both countries. In Angola, the informal market has been used by residents seeking to acquire dollars and dispose of illegal diamond receipts. Since the foreign exchange market was significantly liberalized in 1999, the spread between the official and informal markets has remained below 10 percent. Nigeria has been making progress in liberalizing the multiple exchange rate regime that has been in place since 1994. In response to the rapid decline in international reserves in the first half of 2002, the Nigerian authorities introduced, in July 2002, a Dutch auction system for the primary sale of foreign exchange by the central bank. The objectives of the new system are to safeguard international reserves while allowing the exchange rate to adjust to market conditions. The official exchange rate has depreciated significantly since the auctions have been in place, and the spread between the official rate and the parallel rate has narrowed considerably (to less than 10 percent by end-2002).

C. Discussion and Recommendations

The choice of exchange rate regime is primarily a political decision and cannot easily be based on economic arguments alone. For instance, some participants in the Douala workshop suggested that fixed exchange rates gave the opportunity to eliminate one of the many sources of uncertainty in African economies.

The real exchange rate volatility and appreciation in SSA oil-producing countries, which partly explain the disappointing performance of the non-oil sectors, show that fiscal and monetary policies have not been well adapted to support the chosen exchange rate regime. Structural reforms, as well as improvements in infrastructure and management of public utilities, would also enhance the competitiveness and viability of the non-oil tradable sector in the region.

While structural reforms take time, policymakers should adopt immediately fiscal and monetary policies to safeguard macroeconomic stability and a competitive real exchange rate. In particular, a stable fiscal framework that is delinked from oil market developments would end the boom-bust cycles observed in the past. As outlined in Sections 3 and 4, such a framework would aim at stabilizing expenditure by saving windfall earnings abroad and reducing assets in times of revenue shortfalls. Moreover, foreign savings reduce the need for the domestic sterilization of foreign exchange inflows.

7 Institutional Oversight of the Oil Sector

Background Discussion

In this chapter, we present the structure of institutions that oversee the oil sector. After reviewing the legal framework, we discuss the role of national oil companies.

Legal framework

Countries that have had success in managing their oil sectors usually have a sound legal structure, with a set of laws tailor-made for the oil sector. On the most basic level, the ownership of natural resources—onshore or offshore—is defined. In most countries, a law specifies that the state is the owner of subterranean and sub-marine resources found beyond a certain depth, with private ownership, as in the United States, a rare occurrence. More detailed laws usually govern how and under what type of contract foreign direct investment can be invited to develop oil, and which institution will regulate industry operations. A model contract is often attached to the law, setting out contract terms in general while leaving commercial details open for negotiation. Laws organizing budget operations specify the revenue-collecting institution.

The successful institutional setup normally distinguishes between two tasks in oil sector management: (1) strategic issues regarding the oil industry—for example, the drafting and implementation of legislation, licensing, general contract design, negotiations with foreign investors, and government equity participation; and (2) tactical issues, such as the daily monitoring of oil operations in order to safeguard the appropriate extraction of oil, as well as the social and natural environment. The commercial interests of operators may not always coincide with the interests of the resource owner, and it is therefore important to have an independent regulatory institution.

The technological and financial requirements, as well as the risks involved, mean that most countries have to attract foreign direct investment in order to develop hydrocarbon deposits. Experience has shown that fiscal regimes—that is, the systems that specify the payments due to governments out of oil sales proceeds—differ in their attractiveness to investors and in the level of revenue and risk allocated to the government.[24] Fiscal regimes are sustainable over the long term only if the terms of the agreement, which inevitably have to be drawn up before the potential for hydrocarbon production is known in a given area, are still agreeable once a discovery has been made and production has started. For a fiscal regime to be successful, "fiscal neutrality" is required; that is, the fiscal regime should not have an unwanted influence on the commercial viability of a given hydrocarbon deposit—the main factor in the decision to develop a field—and on the decision to abandon a deposit before the reserves are depleted.

Most countries now use combinations of royalties and profit-based instruments to fulfill the governments' objectives for collecting revenue from project operators (see Box 4).[25] Royalties ensure that the governments receive a minimum payment of revenue from the start of production, irrespective of the project's profitability. Profit-based instruments ensure that the governments reap the benefits of profitable projects. In addition, granting signature bonuses to governments when exploration licenses are being awarded can produce sizable revenue for governments independent of exploration success; also, as very early sunk costs, these bonuses entice companies to move speedily. Finally, oil companies that are incorporated locally—which may be a legal requirement—usually pay corporate income tax.

National oil companies (NOCs)

Governments should evaluate carefully the costs and benefits of NOCs. In very general terms, NOCs are justified in relatively large countries that have the human and financial resources that make a local oil industry a realistic and promising prospect. Adequate conditions have to be created to ensure an effective control over NOCs and international investors by the administration. NOCs should be given the commercial freedom to concentrate on efficiency in producing oil rent, with a clear dividend policy.

---

[24]We prefer to use the term "fiscal regime" rather than taxation. This has been a politically sensitive subject since the nationalization of the oil industry in many countries in the 1970s. The national ownership of resources means that governments see themselves as principals and foreign oil companies as agents that help them develop their resources. The fiscal regime is designed to give incentives to the agents to produce oil efficiently, while leaving as great a share as possible of the proceeds of the oil sales to the resource owner. Taxation, meanwhile, implies that something is taken from companies that would otherwise be theirs.

[25]See Baunsgaard (2001).

Box 4. Production-Sharing Contracts

In many countries, fiscal regimes are codified in production-sharing contracts or agreements (PSCs or PSAs). Under these arrangements, the state retains ownership of the resource and appoints the investor as "contractor" to assist the government in developing the resource. Payment for the contractor is a share of production, and the government will not reimburse the contractor for exploration spending if hydrocarbon deposits do not justify development.

The PSC will usually specify a portion of total production that can be retained by the contractor to recover costs ("cost oil"), while the remainder ("profit oil") is split between the state and the contractor according to a formula set out in the PSC. Royalties or limits on cost oil for any given year ensure some government revenue from the beginning of the project life. In principle, the government receives physical products from the project, but very often agrees on joint marketing with the contractor.

In addition to profit oil, partners in the agreement can be levied petroleum income tax, as well as various forms of bonuses. Recent years have seen large increases of, in particular, signature bonuses payable at the signing of the agreement, and thus not specified in the same. Depending on the setup of the different components, a PSC can be designed to be indistinguishable from a royalty/profit tax combination in financial terms.

Beginning in the 1960s, governments increasingly sought to control oil-extracting activities more directly than through mere legislation and regulation. NOCs were created to accomplish this and to force a faster technology transfer than had been achieved previously. Three arguments can be listed in favor of NOCs. First, the nationalizations of the oil industry in the late 1960s and early 1970s were spectacularly successful in increasing the producers' share of the resource rent. Second, direct national control over production volumes facilitates the management of the worldwide supply and demand balance, whether countries are members of the Organization of Petroleum Exporting Countries (OPEC) or not. With an entirely private oil industry, a government decision to cut production would be more difficult to implement; similarly, private investors would not, like Saudi Arabia, hold the roughly 2 million barrels per day excess capacity that has enabled the country to close sudden supply shortfalls—for example, during the Iranian revolution, the war over Kuwait, or, more recently, the oil sector strike in Venezuela. Third, given the proprietary nature of much of the exploration and development technology, the development of local oil industries probably would not have taken place without forced joint ventures with international technology leaders. Several developing-country NOCs are now technologically on par with the biggest international oil companies (e.g., Petrobras of Brazil and Pemex of Mexico).

However, NOCs pose numerous challenges to the organization and control of the oil sector.[26] Most important, these are related to their unclear position in the principal-agent relationship between the state and the oil industry. The NOC should be the agent that takes part in joint-venture oil projects. Often, it is also the revenue-collection and regulation agent for the state, which makes it the principal vis-à-vis the foreign investors.

In many countries, NOCs have become the vehicle to achieve a broad range of national economic, social, and political objectives, to the detriment of commercial objectives. NOCs have had to create jobs, increase local content of oil sector demand, provide social infrastructure, support regional development, supply transfers through the underpricing of petroleum products, and provide financing for government budgets by borrowing against future oil revenue. The commercial efficiency of NOCs is frequently rated as poor.[27]

Equity participation in oil projects increases government exposure to risk. NOCs have to participate in the financing of exploration activities that may not result in commercial discoveries. The investment needed to develop an oil field may be very large compared with the government budget. Governments, therefore, carry much more of the exploration and reserve risks of oil activities when they participate directly in projects than when they confine themselves to revenue collection.[28]

B. Current Practice

Oil operations in the group are dominated by international oil companies (see Table 8 for a summary of this section). Nevertheless, five out of the seven African oil-producing countries have NOCs. Ministries of finance in these countries are generally in charge of following up on oil revenue payments by the oil companies. All the countries use either production-sharing arrangements (PSAs) or royalty and tax combinations (like the Memoranda of Understanding of Nigeria) to define relations between the government and the oil companies,

---

[26]McPherson (2002).

[27]As an example, McPherson (2002) cites Pertamina of Indonesia, which has operating expenses of $5.50 per barrel of oil, compared with an industry average of $1.20. Another example is SOCAR in Azerbaijan, which in 1999 employed roughly the same number of people as ExxonMobil, even though the latter operated in 100 countries, produced 16 times as much oil, and operated 33 refineries, compared with 2 for SOCAR.

[28]This risk exposure can be mitigated by so-called carried interest, when international investors finance the government's equity share out of future oil revenues; this form of equity participation is equivalent to profit-based fiscal instruments or cost recovery under PSAs (see Sunley, Baunsgaard, and Simard, 2002).

except for Gabon, where some older fields are still operated under concession agreements. Under the PSAs and the royalty/tax contracts, the main sources of government oil revenue are the payment of royalties out of the gross production of oil[29] and the sharing of profits between the state and the oil companies after deductions are made for operating and capital costs.

Contract terms differ widely across countries. The government's share in percent of the total value of production, or the government take, is largest in Nigeria and Cameroon.[30] These countries capture more of the resource rent through the working interest that their NOCs hold in oil fields, which, of course, also means that their governments are exposed to some of the inherent risks of resource exploration. The government's share in Equatorial Guinea is the smallest, partly because the country's three oil fields are in an early phase of development. The fields will produce more government revenue as they mature.

Only Angola and Nigeria have organized competitive bidding rounds to allocate exploration rights; however, some exploration blocks have been allocated to companies on a more ad hoc basis, even in these countries. Angola and Nigeria also receive large initial bonus payments upon approval of new exploration license agreements, and only in these countries are contract terms deemed "international best practice" by industry experts.

Contractual arrangements are often not transparent in the oil-producing countries, as contracts are available only to a small circle of officials and amendments are frequently negotiated—a practice that increases the difficulties of following up on oil revenue. Parliaments are generally not involved in licensing for exploration or development. In some cases, license allocation—and, in all cases, negotiations of contracts—are confidential. In some countries, model production-sharing contracts are readily available (Angola, Cameroon, Equatorial Guinea, and Nigeria). However, model contracts are frequently changed during block allocation negotiations, and the outcome of the negotiations may not be announced publicly. In particular, signature bonus payments are often not included in the PSAs, and transparency is often lacking.

---

[29]Except in ultradeep exploration blocks in Nigeria.

[30]Because of data constraints, we use the government's share in export revenue, rather than the total value of production; given the low ratio of domestic consumption to exports, this is a useful proxy for the African oil-producing countries.

C. Discussion and Recommendations

Participants in the Douala workshop acknowledged that governments often lacked the capacity to oversee effectively the oil sector operations of foreign and national oil companies. One of the problems most often cited was the complex details in oil production contracts. They noted the constructive role NOCs have played in other regions in creating domestic expertise and increasing the government's share of oil revenue. However, they acknowledged that the financial performance of NOCs had been hindered by a lack of a clearly defined purpose, "mission creep," and conflicting demands placed on them by society.

Many participants agreed that NOCs should be allowed to concentrate on maximizing revenue and that administrative units within the government needed to be strengthened in order to meaningfully monitor NOC activities. Technical assistance will be required to achieve better oversight by governments. In some countries, it will also be a challenge to make government positions sufficiently attractive to retain staff once they have been trained, rather than lose them to oil companies.

Governments may lobby the international oil companies operating in their countries to provide technical assistance and training to governments. Often, existing oil production contracts already contain obligations on oil companies to do this; however, these provisions may not have been effectively utilized so far. Discussion should also aim at reducing the complexity of oil production contracts.

Reforms of NOCs' statutes and structures should refocus activities on oil and gas production. Companies should concentrate on their commercial roles, and managers should be evaluated on their commercial achievements. Companies could be subjected to the discipline of financial markets by floating at least a minority share of assets in stock markets, where they exist. Valuation would make it easy to evaluate the performance of managers and policies.

8 Transparency Requirements

Background Discussion

Transparency and accountability in oil sector operations are necessary to improve governance in oil-producing countries. The same transparency and accountability guidelines that apply to non-oil revenue should apply to oil revenue. Oil revenue is part of government budgetary operations, and it is of overwhelming importance in the countries we are dealing with in this paper. The IMF's *Manual on Fiscal Transparency* (IMF, 2001) states that comprehensive coverage of all fiscal activity undertaken by the central government is essential from a transparency standpoint. In some cases, the coverage should extend beyond the government itself: the public sector balance should be reported when nongovernmental public sector agencies undertake significant quasi-fiscal activities. The public should accordingly be provided with full information on the past, current, and projected fiscal activity of the government.

Three concepts of government revenue flows need to be distinguished: (1) payments due, (2) payments made, and (3) payments received. Regarding the first, contractual arrangements between governments and oil companies are usually complex, and payments due to the government are calculated using a multitude of concepts. The most important sources of government revenue in developing countries are royalties (percentages of gross production), production shares (percentages of production net of cost), profit shares (percentages of net project returns), bonuses (fixed, one-off payments due at certain stages of the lifetime of a petroleum reservoir, starting with the signature of the license agreement), and corporate income tax on companies incorporated locally.

Royalties and signature bonuses are easily determined. However, while royalty rates are often publicly available and in some cases contained in basic petroleum legislation, bonuses are agreed upon with individual companies and are usually confidential. Not even royalties are transparent when precise information on production volume is lacking. Similar to bonuses, production shares or profit shares are usually negotiated on a project-by-project basis. The shares due to the government then depend on cost accounting by the project operators and on contractual rules regarding the extent to which costs are tax deductible. Corporate income taxes are paid on net operating profits of companies incorporated locally; these depend on transfer pricing with the company headquarters and are probably the least straightforward of the revenue sources described here.

Regarding the second concept of government revenue flows, revenue payments made to the government, these often differ from payments due. The reasons can be as simple as the accrual of arrears or more complex when offsetting arrangements have been made—for example, when loans have been taken against future oil revenue or oil companies provide goods and services to the government in lieu of cash payments. It is essential that government departments and agencies charged with monitoring the oil sector and managing oil fiscal revenues put in place adequate control mechanisms that allow them to reconcile payments due and payments received on a continuous basis. Equally important is the need to phase out those practices that hinder effective budget control and central cash management by the treasury, such as earmarking specific oil revenues for financing expenditures in a way that bypasses established budget control procedures.

Finally, with respect to the third concept of government revenue flows, payments in most countries are made to more than one administrative unit. They can go to an international bank, a national bank, the NOC, and different ministries. Payments are also frequently made to foreign bank accounts in foreign currency (usually the U.S. dollar); repatriation of the payments then depends on the central bank. In particular, when an NOC participates in oil sector operations, this filters at least some of the revenue payments made, and the pass-through to the treasury is not always straightforward. Payments made and payments received by the treasury need to be reconciled regularly.

Transparency in oil sector operations is needed to allow democratic debate on fiscal policy and spending priorities. Verification mechanisms and enhanced accountability are instrumental for avoiding corruption and the waste of public resources. Transparency is also needed to allow forward planning. An argument often used against transparency in oil sector operations is that spending pressure will build up from disclosures about resource availability (for example, it is forbidden by law to disclose the value of foreign assets accumulated in Kuwait, because such a disclosure is feared to generate spending pressure). However, it would seem better to inform the public and foster constructive debate. The existence of oil resources cannot be kept secret, and spending pressure will mount when citizens have little confidence in public institutions.

The question is how to make oil revenue information available to the public. A credible aggregation of the payments due to the government needs to be made, for the following reasons: (1) the multitude of concepts means that the fiscal authorities often do not have the capacity to follow up on oil revenue due, in particular in countries with a large number of oil-producing companies; (2) transparency is difficult to achieve when the public cannot easily understand the nature and origin of government revenue, even if it were to be made public; and (3) insofar as contractual details are negotiated on an individual basis, they are usually protected by confidentiality clauses. These considerations argue in favor of simplifying or standardizing fiscal arrangements and presenting information in a way that can be understood.

Fiscal operations in the oil sector should be subjected to independent scrutiny. Foreign oil companies are usually required to make regular declarations to the government of their contractual payments and submit audited account statements at the end of each year. Independent auditing of their adherence to contracts and payments of oil revenue, performed by the government, should verify the companies' declarations and compare them with assessments and payments received. The government auditor should also check the activities of the revenue-assessing and -collecting agencies and prepare timely and trustworthy reports on the financial integrity of government accounts—including oil revenue. The multitude of concepts involved means that the fiscal authorities often do not have the capacity to follow up on oil revenue due, in particular in countries with a large number of oil-producing companies. In order to help governments become more transparent, administrative capacity in oil sector operations needs to be strengthened in most African countries.

To establish transparency in fiscal operations related to the oil sector, an administrative unit is needed that is trustworthy in the public's eye and technically capable of handling the complex tasks involved in the follow-up of oil revenue. Depending on country circumstances, this can take very different forms. In most of the SSA oil-exporting countries, the public has less than full confidence in government agencies, and administrative capacity is generally low. The creation of a new unit may therefore be necessary.

In countries where fiscal accounts are generally trustworthy and well presented, the unit could be created within the treasury or ministry of finance and could consist of a number of tax and customs officials under the overview of the minister of finance. In many countries, more officials would be needed. Where governance concerns are strong and the public has come to mistrust officials and institutions, we could envisage an independent authority, with a board of governors that includes finance and oil ministers, the central bank governor, and representatives of civil society and oil companies.

In addition, the international oil companies operating in the countries could take steps to improve transparency. As argued recently by a broad coalition of civil society groups, international oil companies should open their books and publish what they pay to governments, with the hope that this would immediately increase the pressure upon these governments to account for the uses made of the oil revenue payments.[31] In September 2002, U.K. Prime Minister Tony Blair launched the Extractive Industries Transparency Initiative (EITI), which encouraged governments, public and private companies, international organizations, and others with an interest in these industries to work together and voluntarily develop a framework to promote the transparency of payments and revenues arising from extractive natural resources.[32] Adopting the initiative's approach to promoting transparency and the prudent use of extractive revenues would help in achieving sustainable economic growth and development in countries dependent on these resources.

At Evian, in June 2003, the Group of Eight (G-8) industrialized nations expressed support for the EITI, reaffirming their commitment "to fight corruption more effectively, including a specific initiative on extractive industries." The G-8 also suggested a role for the IMF and other multilaterals. It encouraged governments and companies to disclose information on revenue flows and payments from the extractive industries to an agreed third party, such as the IMF or the World Bank. The G-8 also encouraged the IMF and the World Bank to give technical support to the governments participating in the EITI. Since its launch, the initiative has developed into a multi-stakeholder group. At the first EITI conference in London, Nigeria and São Tomé and Príncipe pledged to participate in the EITI and to publish the financial results of their next licensing rounds.

B. Current Practice

In all the countries in the group, oil sector operations lack transparency and suffer from institutional capacity constraints (Table 8). Although there are variations, in general arrangements among the treasuries, the ministries in charge of the oil sector and the NOCs, where they exist, are not clearly defined; the government institutions in charge of the oil sector lack human resources; and data provision is not adequate to allow for a comprehensive monitoring of oil revenue. Oil companies usually provide information on export liftings to ministries, and NOCs are informed automatically if they hold a working interest in a field. However, ministries in charge of the oil sector are frequently not in charge of government revenue collection and therefore do not pass on information to the finance ministries or the treasuries.

---

[31]See www.publishwhatyoupay.org

[32]See www.dfid.gov.uk

Box 5. Does Governance Matter?

There is now a general consensus that poor governance, corruption, and lack of transparency are major obstacles to effective policymaking, economic growth, poverty alleviation, and good economic performance generally. Promoting good governance and strengthening institutions are recognized to be urgent responsibilities of governments, aided by international, regional, and nongovernmental organizations. In view of the importance of the role of good governance and as mandated by the Interim Committee in September 1996, the IMF addresses governance issues with all member countries, including African countries, where such issues are relevant.

There are many acceptable definitions of governance. A common meaning of the term would be the act or the process of being governed. In the case of countries, governance would be the role of the government, its policies, and the diverse range of its activities and practices. If we consider only economic governance, it would involve transparency, good economic and financial management, and accountability by the state (Wolf and Gürgen, 2000).

While it is easy to agree on the desirability of good governance, we are here interested in empirical evidence linking governance to development indicators. In a recent study, Kaufmann, Kraay, and Zoido-Lobatón (1999) group governance indicators into six clusters: Voice and Accountability, Political Instability and Violence, Government Effectiveness, Regulatory Burden, Rule of Law, and Graft. Using these six clusters over a cross section of more than 150 countries, the authors produce new empirical evidence of a strong causal relationship between improved governance and three better development outcomes: per capita income, infant mortality, and increase in literacy. From these results, the authors conclude: "governance matters."

One important manifestation of poor governance is corruption. Much empirical evidence shows that corruption adversely affects growth (Wolf and Gürgen, 2000). It is a significant force inhibiting investment and discouraging foreign donors. Corruption also has costs "in terms of the deterioration in the quality of the existing infrastructure. These costs can be very high in terms of their impact on growth" (Tanzi and Davoodi, 1997). Another empirical study by Mauro (1997) presents "regression analysis to show that the amount of corruption is negatively linked to the level of investment and economic growth, that is to say, the more corruption, the less investment and the less economic growth." Corruption imposes a heavy burden on the most innovative and most productive segments of the economy—the small and medium-sized enterprises. And corruption hits the poor particularly hard since they cannot afford to pay bribes.

In sum, given the accumulating evidence of a strong correlation among good governance, economic growth, and economic welfare, good governance can be considered to be an essential building block of a country's economic success.

In some countries, different branches of the government are in charge of different types of oil revenue. In Nigeria, receipts from direct sales of crude oil are channeled through the NOC, royalties are collected by the Department of Petroleum Resources, and petroleum profit taxes are collected by the Federal Inland Revenue Service. Where there is an NOC, government oil revenue flows pass through the company accounts, and deposits in treasury accounts depend on the dividend policy of the NOC, at least for those oil fields in which the NOC has an active working interest. In fields without NOC participation, the NOC may nevertheless market the government's share of production, while the proceeds from the marketing are transferred to the treasury (e.g., in the Republic of Congo). This practice can introduce a time lag between accrual and payment of government oil revenue, which further reduces transparency in oil sector operations. Carried interest (the financing of the NOC's share in the investment costs of an oil field by other investors in the field) is another obstacle to transparency, insofar as it implies contingent liabilities that may be difficult to quantify. This situation is further complicated by financial agreements subsequently made with private oil companies. In the Republic of Congo, for instance, the liabilities of the national oil company, the SNPC, from carried interest have been subject to swapping arrangements between private oil companies and the government, through which the government has agreed to reduce its future claims on these companies in exchange for a reduction in their claims on the SNPC. The role delineation between the NOC and the treasury can easily become blurred if the NOC's dividend and investment policy is not clearly defined (as in the Republic of Congo), or if the NOC is directly involved in financing public expenditure without the funds used passing through the treasury.

Operations of foreign oil companies are audited by independent external auditors in most countries, although the auditing may not always be in line with international auditing standards. Operations of NOCs are audited only in some cases. Audits of foreign oil companies were conducted in Equatorial Guinea for the first time at end-2000, and the authorities contracted with the auditors to perform annual audits henceforth. In Gabon, audits were called for under the now-lapsed Stand-By Arrangement but were not initiated until March 2002. In addition to the independent external financial audits, a detailed operational and managerial audit was recently carried out in Cameroon. The conducting of a financial audit of the SNPC in the Republic of Congo by an independent, internationally recognized auditing firm in conformity with international auditing standards is one of the structural benchmarks under the staff-monitored program.[33] Government accounts are generally not audited, although some of the countries conduct public expenditure reviews, usually with support from the World Bank.

---

[33]Financial audits can play a useful role only if NOCs prepare regular financial statements, with proper coverage and based on proper accounting.

Table 8. Current Practice in Governance and Transparency

Country	National Oil Companies	Production Sharing	Bidding Rounds	Contract Transparency	Audits	Data Availability
Angola	Yes, Sonangol.	The latest generation of Angolan production-sharing agreements (PSAs) is regarded as "international best practices."	Award of new blocks, in principle, through a competitive bidding process but recent licensing rounds have not been transparent.	No.	No independent audit of Sonangol available. Tax payments by foreign oil companies are audited regularly. But audits are not made public.	Insufficient. Data on contracts, audits, net tax liability of Sonangol etc. not available.
Cameroon	Yes, Société Nationale des Hydrocarbures (SNH).	Yes.	No.	Yes.	Independent audits of SNH being conducted annually.	Under the PRGF-supported program the authorities are committed to report monthly data related to oil sector operations.
Chad	No, but the government is a partner in a joint venture with foreign oil companies that manages the export pipeline.	Yes.	No.	Yes.	Audits are to be conducted annually of oil revenue payments, of offshore accounts that receive oil payments, and of spending financed by oil revenue.	Under the PRGF-supported program the authorities are committed to report monthly data related to oil sector operations.
Republic of Congo	Yes, SNPC.	Yes.	No.	Yes.	The World Bank has offered financial and technical support for the operational audit of the petroleum sector and the SNPC. Audits have not yet been conducted.	Insufficient.

Table 8 (concluded)

Country	National Oil Companies	Production Sharing	Bidding Rounds	Contract Transparency	Audits	Data Availability
Equatorial Guinea	Yes, Gepetrol. Established in 2001 and expected to take working interest in any new oil projects.	A model PSA is posted on the website of the Ministry of Mining. The details of taxation are negotiated. The percentage of government oil revenue is low by international comparison.	No.	Bilateral negotiations between companies and government not transparent. PSAs remain confidential and not discussed outside small circle in Ministry of Mining and the Presidency.	Audits of oil company operations and government oil revenue payments undertaken for the first time in 2001 and reports made available to IMF staff.	Insufficient. Data on government bank deposits abroad and on oil exports and government oil revenue are not available. Also, information on borrowing against future oil revenues not transparent.
Gabon	None.	Most fields are operated under PSAs, but some older license regimes persist.	No.	No.	Audits of three smaller oil companies were completed in end-2001 while those for the two largest companies and two smaller ones were initiated and completed in September 2002.	Insufficient. There is no systematic comparison by the authorities of data available on (1) tax payments; (2) tax declaration by companies; and (3) tax obligations assessed and controlled by the Tax Department.
Nigeria	Yes, NNPC.	Used since 1991 to encourage deepwater and inland basin exploration, although production is still marginal. A standard model contract was published in 1993.	In principle, but with a lack of transparency. Some ad hoc allocation of blocks persists.	Yes.	Tax audits of oil companies seem to be ineffective. Frequency of audits of the oil sector is inadequate.	Insufficient.

Sources: Country authorities; and IMF staff analyses.

Box 6. Oil Sector Operations in Cameroon—Improvements in Transparency Under the PRGF

The national oil company (SNH) was created in 1980, under the aegis of the Secretary General at the Presidency, to receive payments from, and make payments to, oil companies for operations related to oil exploration and exploitation. The SNH is also responsible for negotiating and supervising the partnership agreements concluded with private oil companies, as well as marketing and selling the government's share of oil output and transferring oil revenue to the treasury.

Before the implementation of the Poverty Reduction and Growth Facility (PRGF)-supported program, a lack of transparency was manifested, notably by extrabudgetary government operations financed directly by the SNH, as well as tax evasion by private oil companies through tax loopholes. In recent years, the government has made noticeable progress in consolidating transparency and accountability in the sector:

• The SNH, which previously reported directly to the president of Cameroon, now transfers oil revenue to the national budget on a timely basis. An automatic transfer mechanism was worked out in December 1999 between the Ministry of Finance and the SNH, with the assistance of the World Bank and IMF staff. Under this mechanism, regular meetings are held between the technical monitoring committee for the government's program (CTS) and SNH officials to review the company's cash-flow position on the basis of actual data on production, exports, international oil prices, and exchange rates, and to agree on the timing of the transfers to the budget.

• Independent audits of the SNH have been conducted as part of the IMF-supported program since 1998 by international auditing firms. The harmonization of the accounting system of the SNH with international norms was implemented with the assistance of Ernst and Young in mid-2000. The SNH was able to produce for the first time financial statements for end-June 2001 in accordance with international accounting standards. This new accounting system will allow the company to provide accounts on a real-time basis and financial statements every six months. The government is determined to ensure that the SNH completes the installation of its upgraded financial management and accounting system in order to avoid a return to old accounting practices.

• An operational and organizational audit of the SNH has been completed, its recommendations adopted, and a reform strategy formulated in early 2001. Among the recommendations of the action plan, the government intends, by end 2002, to (1) redefine the respective roles and responsibilities of the private and public sector in the oil industry and provide a timetable for the implementation of the reform program; and (2) provide a strategy and an action plan for promoting private sector investment in the hydrocarbon sector.

Regular data on general government revenue and expenditure—including oil revenue—are available in only about half of the oil-producing countries. Most countries suffer from an insufficient follow-up of oil revenues by treasury officials, while in some countries accounts between finance ministries and NOCs are not reconciled.

C. Discussion and Recommendations

Poor governance and lack of transparency have been a major concern in oil-producing countries in sub-Saharan Africa. They are a major factor contributing to these countries' apparent inability to benefit from the ample availability of extractive resources. Indeed, such resource endowment is now often seen as a "resource curse."

Some participants in the Douala workshop felt that calls for greater transparency often did not properly acknowledge the improvements already made. Also, they cautioned against publication of information with regard to oil receipts as this could lead to spending pressures and even pose dangers to political stability. They felt that they needed to be cautious in disseminating information, so as to avoid unreasonable expectations and confusion, especially when oil revenues fall short of budgetary projections due to unforeseen events. Participants stressed the weak administrative capacity of their governments and, in particular, the lack of skills and resources in statistical agencies to provide adequate data on the oil sector. They also felt restricted by the confidentiality clauses in the existing contracts.

It will therefore be necessary to strengthen skills and resources in statistical agencies and to strengthen administrative capacity in general. In these areas, international institutions like the IMF and the World Bank can provide technical assistance. However, it is important that the governments of oil-producing countries create a more transparent environment. It is equally important that oil companies promote transparency in their transactions with the oil-exporting countries by, among other things, agreeing to reduce the requirements for confidentiality in their contracts. Governments and oil companies could therefore agree on greater transparency, as proposed under the EITI. Good governance and transparency have the potential of helping African oil-exporting countries increase revenues, which could then be used for much-needed development and poverty reduction. Ultimately, success in these countries also serves the interests of international oil companies, because it will show that they can avert the reputational and operational risks they face in these circumstances.

9 Final Discussion: Toward an Agenda for Further Work

The fact that oil-producing countries in Africa have not achieved better social indicators than other African countries gives rise to the question of whether this was despite or because of the inflow of billions of U.S. dollars in foreign investment in oil installations, and government oil revenue. The persistent underachievement of development goals has come to be seen as the "resource curse." This paper has shown, however, that macroeconomic policies and governance can be designed in a way that turn oil revenue into a "blessing."

SSA oil-exporting countries have so far not implemented adequate policies for using their resources effectively. Fiscal and monetary policies have not served to stabilize the economies in light of oil revenue volatility, exchange rates have been allowed to be a burden on the non-oil sector, and the depletion of the natural resource has not been balanced by an accumulation of income-generating assets that would benefit future generations. Moreover, administrative capacity constraints and institutional setups have created an opaque environment that has been more conducive to illicit appropriation of oil rents by private individuals than to the rational, effective use of oil revenue for the benefit of the populations.

Good macroeconomic policies and governance form the core of what is needed to turn oil revenue into a blessing for oil-exporting countries in Africa. The discussions during the Douala workshop have clearly shown that African policymakers agree with this assessment. To move forward, action needs to be taken in three areas:

First, governments and oil companies should improve transparency in the oil sector by regularly providing information on oil sector activities to policymakers, to the IMF, and to the public. The information provided to the public does not need to be as detailed as the information needed for policymaking; however, a way needs to be found to make the aggregated data credible to a population made skeptical by long-standing governance concerns.

Second, policy discussions should be initiated within the oil-exporting countries, with as broad a participation as feasible, about oil revenue management in general and the government's spending priorities in particular. The aim would be to identify the level of spending that is feasible without endangering macroeconomic stability and wasting resources, to inform the population of constraints and possibilities, to decide on a fiscal rule to guide government spending, and to decide on an asset investment strategy for the accumulation of savings. Broad participation would help in ensuring ownership of the resulting policies.

Third, weaknesses in national capacities for the design of effective spending programs and oil sector oversight should be identified and technical assistance mobilized from multilateral institutions, bilateral donors, and international oil companies operating in Africa.

There is a great need to continue discussions, at both the international and national levels, to enhance understanding and ownership of policies and ensure widespread support for chosen policy directions. A workshop similar to Douala is planned by the IMF and the World Bank, to which will be invited not only high-level officials of oil-exporting countries but also representatives of international oil companies. Furthermore, governments should explore the possibilities for organizing national stakeholder discussions, possibly with the participation of the IMF, the World Bank, and other donors.

As international interest in African oil rises, so do the frustration and impatience of the populations in oil-exporting countries, who see their aspirations thwarted by problems of underdevelopment despite the apparent riches flowing from the oil wells. Increasingly, populations demand major improvements in economic policies, transparency, accountability, and public service delivery.

References

Barnett, Steven, and Rolando Ossowski, 2002, "Operational Aspects of Fiscal Policy in Oil-Producing Countries," IMF Working Paper 02/177 (Washington: International Monetary Fund).

Baunsgaard, Thomas, 2001, "A Primer on Mineral Taxation," IMF Working Paper 01/139 (Washington: International Monetary Fund).

Bjerkholt, Olav, 2002, "Fiscal Rules for Economies with Non-Renewable Resources," paper prepared for the conference "Rules-Based Fiscal Policies in Emerging Market Economies," Oaxaca, Mexico, February.

Daniel, James, 2001, "Hedging Government Oil Price Risk," IMF Working Paper 01/185 (Washington: International Monetary Fund).

Engel, Eduardo, and Rodrigo Valdés, 2000, "Optimal Fiscal Strategy for Oil-Exporting Countries," IMF Working Paper 00/118 (Washington: International Monetary Fund).

Hausmann, Ricardo, and Roberto Rigobon, 2002, "An Alternative Interpretation of the Resource Curse: Theory and Policy Implications for Stabilization, Saving, and Beyond," paper presented at the IMF Conference on Fiscal Policy Formulation and Implementation in Oil-Producing Countries, Washington, June 5–6.

International Monetary Fund, 2001, *Manual on Fiscal Transparency* (Washington).

Kaufmann, Daniel, Art Kraay, and Pablo Zoido-Lobatón, 1999, "Governance Matters," World Bank Policy Research Working Paper No. 2196 (Washington: World Bank).

Laidler, David, 1999, "The Exchange Rate Regime and Canada's Monetary Order," Working Paper No. 99-7 (Ottawa: Bank of Canada).

Mauro, Paolo, 1997, *Why Worry About Corruption?* IMF Economic Issues No. 6 (Washington: International Monetary Fund).

McPherson, Charles, 2002, "National Oil Companies: Evolution, Issues, Outlook," paper presented at the IMF Conference on Fiscal Policy Formulation and Implementation in Oil-Producing Countries, Washington, June 5–6.

Reinhart, Carmen, and Kenneth Rogoff, 2002, "The Modern History of Exchange Rate Arrangements: A Reinterpretation," NBER Working Paper

No. 8963 (Cambridge, Massachusetts: National Bureau of Economic Research).

Sunley, Emil M., Thomas Baunsgaard, and Dominique Simard, 2002, "Revenue from Oil and Gas Sector: Issues and Country Experience," paper presented at the IMF Conference on Fiscal Policy Formulation and Implementation in Oil-Producing Countries, Washington, June 5–6.

Tanzi, Vito, and Hamid R. Davoodi, 1997, "Corruption, Public Investment, and Growth," IMF Working Paper 97/139 (Washington: International Monetary Fund).

Wolf, Thomas, and Emine Gürgen, 2000, *Improving Governance and Fighting Corruption in the Baltic and CIS Countries: The Role of the IMF*, IMF Economic Issues No. 21 (Washington: International Monetary Fund).